In the Shadow of Danger
ARMY LIFE-STORIES

In the Shadow of Danger
ARMY LIFE-STORIES

Gautam Banerjee

PENTAGON PRESS

In the Shadow of Danger: Army Life-stories / *Gautam Banerjee*

First Published in 2014

ISBN 978-81-8274-795-1

Published by
PENTAGON PRESS
206, Peacock Lane, Shahpur Jat
New Delhi-110049
Phones: 011-64706243, 26491568
Telefax: 011-26490600
email: rajan@pentagonpress.in
website: www.pentagonpress.in

Branch:
Prime Arcade
Office #11
1154 Saifee Street
Opp. M.G.Road, Camp
Pune-411001
Email: pentagonpresspune@gmail.com

Printed at Avantika Printers Private Limited.

CONTENTS

AUTHOR'S NOTE

Reading – and sometimes, writing – has been a traditional engagement for the army officers during their long years of living in areas remote from civilisation, family and friends. It provides a ground for normal human feelings to play, unencumbered by the strict demeanour of leadership that one is obliged to display at all times. It helps one in keeping his humour.

I was no exception but for the uncertain distinction of having had more opportunities than most to spend time alone and away. Obviously, I took to writing on whatever took my fancy.

Nothing must remain out of a commander's knowledge. Soon therefore, my 'notes', as these were referred to, found favour with my superior officers, who while tasking me to prepare more and more official papers, training pamphlets, reports and so on, also encouraged me to keep writing.

This book is a compilation of stories penned down at intermittent intervals over the forty years that I had the privilege of donning the army uniform. All of these are real-life, true stories, though many times the narratives have either been exaggerated or eased down in the interest of readability. Photographs have come from my own camera – I had been an avid photographer, limited in skill though as the reader may notice. It may also be appreciated that it is neither a literary work nor a 'thinkers' thesis – a soldier's calling needs different kinds of accomplishments. Indeed, it is just a soldier's narration of certain episodes that he found worth recording.

I hope the reading would give at least a fraction of the joy that it gave me penning it.

Gautam Banerjee

1

First Blood: East Pakistan 1971

The twenty year old Second Lieutenant looked up to the dark November night sky, "I might not be there to gaze upon these eternal companions of mankind ever again", he thought. He recalled his grandma fascinating him in their open courtyard with after-dinner tales of the constellations like the *Saptarishi* etc. and weaving stories around them as he lay nestled in her bosom. "After their time in *martyalok* is over, all good humans find place among the congregation of stars. Your grandfather and everyone else of our departed family are there, keeping an eternal watch over their progeny", she would explain. Thus was built up a sort of bondage between him and the stars. Presently, however, it seemed a bit amusing to picture that he might not be around a few hours hence while everything else would go on as usual.

The infantry battalion was tasked to capture *Bhurungamari*, a largish village few kilometres across the Indo-East Pakistan border where a strong defended locality was held by a company of the 25 PUNJAB Battalion of the Pakistan Army, duly supported by the usual complements of the 'Rajakars' and the 'East Pakistan Civil Armed Forces'. It was just past six in the evening when the rifle company commander's final verbal orders for the attack were concluded.

Earlier, he had attended the battalion commander's orders when assault tasks for his field platoon of engineers had been spelt out. Following the hoary dictates of 'battle procedure', he now proceeded to brief his field platoon as to what each section and soldier had to do and how. That was the last moment when he could let his mind wander; hereafter there was just the 'objective', the tactics of capturing it, and resolute combat action regardless, nothing else, to occupy the mind. He was no more an individual being but just one cog in a humungous war machine.

The 'H Hour', the time to commence the attack, was fixed at 2359 hours. Before that there would be the tactical move of assaulting troops to the 'Forming Up Place' from where the enemy positions at Bhurungamari East and Bhurungamari West would be attacked. Of course, the entire duration of combat would be supported by own artillery fire, while the enemy would use all its weapons, its artillery on the lead, to break up the attack. Bhurungamari East, if captured, would allow the battalion to tackle the rest of the Pakistan Army positions from the rear. As sporadic shelling by the enemy carried on throughout the day, he briefed and rehearsed his platoon before grouping one of his sections each with the 'Bravo' and 'Charlie' Companies which were to assault in Phase I, and retained the rest of the platoon with the battalion commander's group.

The battalion moved off to the Forming Up Place at 2000 hours. He knew the terrain well, having accompanied the patrols that were sent out over the past three nights to reconnoitre the 'no-man's land' and to select a suitable 'Forming Up Place' and its alternative. Amused and excited at the prospect of fighting a battle, he recalled the events during the first patrol when a cool, thirty year old veteran Major who was leading the patrol, by his fool-hardy courage and an itch for a fight – an innate urge that pervades among young officers – had landed the group in trouble. The Major had set up a clash with a Pakistani patrol which was passing by unaware of their presence. Having taken what they considered to be a good position to ambush the enemy, they had been surprised by another detachment of the enemy appearing behind them. Finding no cover from that direction, they had lain still, ready to leap out and engage in a certain-death fight, when, curiously, the enemy had moved away! The Major, however, wasn't yet done. Having completed the patrol task, the patrol had started on their return route when the Major decided to find out more about the enemy positions. The method chosen to do so was to provoke the enemy to open fire, a lucrative target being offered by the glow of cigarettes lit by the Major and he standing on a high embankment which had supported a road before the partition divided the land. Sadly, the enemy did not oblige.

The very next night, another patrol leader, a happy and boisterous Captain, had taken position at a patrol base close to the enemy defences to help him reconnoitre for mines. Inching towards the enemy position, he had suddenly found himself and his batman-buddy prone close to a Pakistani bunker, light from a hurricane lantern finding escape from its loop holes. Realising his stupidity in going up so close, the duo had quietly crawled back inch by inch, an excursion complicated by the resolve to carry back those three mines that they had recovered from the mine field covering the Pakistani positions. They must have made some noise, for the enemy had opened fire in their direction. The Captain had then moved to one flank and responded with counter-fire to draw the enemy's attention away from the pinned down duo.

Assaulting deliberately prepared defences was, however, all together a different matter. It was a clash of supreme 'will', courage and quick wit, attributes the GRENADIERS seem to have in ample measure. Anticipating the attack on Bhurungamari East to be more crucial, he joined up with the 'Charlie' Company which had the intrepid Major in command. The attack commenced dot on time. His engineer troops had been grouped with the assaulting rifle platoons and thus having nothing challenging to do for the time being, he joined one of the attacking sections in running over three bunkers one after the other, at the end finding himself at the 'objective' specified. By 0300 hours, Bhurungamari East had been captured, and the Company got busy in reorganising itself. Meanwhile, battle raged on at its Western part till 0730 hours when 'Bravo' Company finally captured it.

As dawn broke, there was detected another set of defensive positions between these two captured positions which, now reinforced with the fugitives from the fallen positions, threatened to unhinge the attack. With the other two companies – 'Alfa' and 'Delta' – well on their way to the Phase II attack, the tall, balding and unassuming battalion commander now decided to clear this gap between his two companies – he attacked with what troops he could find from the battalion headquarters. Ordered to gather the rest of his platoon – which, reinforced with 'reservists', had swollen to nearly double the regular strength – he was placed in command of a mixed group of soldiers to leap-frog astride the abandoned road, till they hit the first line of Pakistani bunkers. Only one bunker had to be fought for, the rest were abandoned but for dead enemy soldiers. Proceeding further, the group found itself among more enemy defences, all silent but for an occasional burst of fire coming from here and there. Soon, he linked up with the rest of the battalion headquarters troops who had established contact with the companies on the East and the West. Pakistani forward positions and its company headquarters had been captured and Phase I was complete by 1000 hours, four hours past the expected time of completion.

Parties were assigned to find the wounded and carry them back to the erstwhile Forming Up Place where the 'Medical Aid Post' was now located. And then came the solemn event: collection of dead soldiers – those who were his comrades till a few hours back and those whom he saw as enemy even if he knew them not. Under sporadic shelling from Pakistani positions further away, the Company Havildar Major got busy in preparing inventories of the bodies and their possessions, to be sent back to the Record Office and to the next-of-kin, and cremating and burying these colleagues as well as enemies with as much honour that could be accorded under the circumstances. By this time, however, he had moved off with another patrol to establish contact with the next enemy position.

A twenty year old Second Lieutenant had matured at that instant.

*

2

Olive Green in 'Dev-Bhoomi'

On to 'Dev-Bhoomi'!

It was in March 1972 when we moved from the new-born nation of Bangladesh back to our pre-1971 War location, Joshimath in the Garhwal Hills of what was then a part of Uttar Pradesh and now forms part of the state of Uttarakhand.

During the War, the Chinese, in solidarity with their long time lackey, had invented an instance of 'Indian intrusion' or some such 'provocation' across what they claimed to be the Sino-Indian Border – Tibetan territory actually that they had integrated into the Communist China in 1951 – and 'warned' India in their typical rhetorical style. The high Himalayan passes along the Indo-Tibet Border being 'closed' with deep snow cover, the Chinese could do little to distract India during the December 1971 War. But as the summer of 1972 dawned, there were apprehensions that even if too late, the Chinese might create some trouble to assuage their friend's ignominious defeat, and grab some territorial possessions for themselves in the process.

The Joshimath Sector, having a number of important religious shrines was aptly referred to as the 'Dev-Bhoomi' (abode of God), and was considered as a value objective for such mischief. Accordingly, army units located in that Sector were activated in brisk reconnaissance, planning and preparation of field fortifications. With that purpose, a series of long-range patrols had been launched, with the task of building up detailed terrain data and examine various tactical options to resist any Chinese incursion; the operation was codenamed 'Operation HORNET'[1].

This narrative is a description of the scenes and the surroundings that one was fortunate to savour during one of the priority long-range patrols. On account of the nature of the task, these patrols had to be of long-durations, and gave one much time to establish intimacy with the land. Notably, the description is recorded along the journey upwards, from the plains of Hardwar to the Indo-Tibet Border Pass of Mana situated at an altitude of 18,500 feet or so – in other words, against the run of the rivers and in alignment with a visitor from the plains of Hardwar.

Joshimath

In February 1972, we found Joshimath to be a small township of tightly packed dwellings clinging to the steep mountainous slope and served by narrow cobbled lanes. Houses had thick walls made of stone tablets of rough rectangular shape and piled in layers with mud-mortar bonding, while doors and windows were made of exquisitely carved timber battens and planks that were held together by hand-beaten iron clamps. Tiles of slate-stone, supported by timber beams and runners, made for the traditional roof though a preference for corrugated iron sheet roofing was evident.

Till the early 1960's, Joshimath was connected with Hardwar-Raiwala via Rishikesh, Devprayag, Rudraprayag and Karnaprayag by a narrow and difficult one way road. Each of the aforementioned 'prayag' signified the union of two tributaries of the River Ganga and therefore, according to Hindu tradition, a sacred spot.[2] Starting from Hardwar where the River Ganga burst out into the vast Gangetic Plains, the single road ran all along the upstream course of its sacred tributaries till its terminus at

Joshimath. By the late 1960's the road had been developed to one-way military Class 9 specifications, much to the pride of the people and relief of the pilgrims who journeyed to Badrinath Dham and Kedarnath to fulfil a sacred Hindu ordination, obligatory more or less. Even then, the 280 kilometre journey from Raiwala to Joshimath took two to three days to perform.

The road bisects Joshimath town East-West, leaving the ancient Narsingh-Durga Temple[3] and the core residential area to its down-slope side and runs beyond till it branches off on the downhill side towards the most revered Hindu shrine of Badrinath, 45 kilometres to the North. The other branch continues straight East towards Malari, a nondescript summer village 90 kilometres distant whose significance lay in its tactical situation that was vital to keep one sector of the Indo-Tibet Border secure.[4]

The uphill side of the road is occupied by the Army with some civilian settlements nestled between till it flattenes out to merge into a beautiful meadow named Auli.[5] Just above the old town is the school, an army helipad and hospital. The Jyotir Math (seminary) – an ancient cave with a mulbury tree known as the 'Kalapavriksha' (salvation tree) over it – is also located just above the town. It is here that Adi Guru Shankaracharya got his enlightenment in the 8th Century C.E. before he revived the tradition of Badrinath 'Dham' (destination Badrinath, a religious undertaking for the Hindus, binding more or less) and consecrated the shrine where it stands today. And it is along that road bisecting the two sides of the town where the Joshimath life thrives: a chaotic cluster of shops, sweetmeat sellers, loitering pilgrims, blaring music devotional as well as raunchy, photographic studios displaying black and white photographs of local youngsters in various poses, gossiping groups, chaotic bus stand, and so on.

Badrinath Dham

The road from Joshimath to Badrinath Dham starts with a long loop over steep downhill slope till it hits the left bank of River Alaknanda. At this spot, River Dhauli Ganga runs down from Malari in the North-East to meet River Alaknanda, the confluence being known as Vishnu Prayag. Crossing over a longish bridge which is distinguished by its fate of getting washed away every decade or so, the road heads towards Govind Ghat from where takes off a tedious track to the famous Sikh pilgrimage destination of Hemkund Sahib. The road also runs by Pandukeshwar, the village where legend says the Pandavas had stayed on their journey to the Heaven after completing their assigned term in the 'mrityu-lok' (this, transitory world). Then, after an hour and a half long journey of awe-inspiring twists and turns, appears the small seasonal settlement of Hanuman Chatti. Like all other pilgrim destinations, Badrinath Dham too has a penultimate halt at here. On arrival at this spot, the pilgrims are liable to be elated in having overcome the rigours of a tough journey and being filled with anticipation of the impending 'darshan' (holy see) of the Lord. Few eateries selling hot tea and variety of snacks add to the joyous atmosphere. In the middle of the hum-drum stands a temple that basks in Badrinath's glory, offering a preview of the greater religious opportunity to come.

Negotiating another steep, nerve-raking climb under a half-tunnel, the road bursts out into the wide valley of the River Alaknanda which cradles the Badrinath Temple. The altitude here is above 10,000 feet. Going along, one was rewarded with a sight majestic and fulfilling: a gushing River Alaknanda, the Temple complex standing out on its right bank in the backdrop of snow covered, cone shaped Mount Neel Kantha, and religious 'akharas' (compounds), 'dharamshalas' (pilgrim huts) and a market on the opposite bank. The road continued a couple of kilometres to terminate at Village Mana before the great Himalayan heights put a stop to habitation. Mana was the last settlement of the locals, the hardy and handsome Bhotia's, albeit inhabited only during the summer months.

The tradition of Bradrinath Dham is a long narrative and quite well known. It would therefore suffice to mention here that the Shrine is approached over a foot bridge and after a climb over some stairs, is entered through an ornate gateway that is set into a colourfully painted facade made of timber and stone. A court yard lies ahead, at the centre of which is the sanctum sanctorum of the Lord. The Lord's image is a flattish stone tablet of trapezoidal shape which may be beholden only during the early morning ritual of 'abhishek' (annotation), remaining obscured by embellishments at other times. The presiding priest, referred to as the 'Rawal', is a chosen one from the ancient clan of distinguished priests of Southern India – a tradition coming down from the time of Shakaracharya. It is he who is ordained to perform the complex rituals daily in the early mornings and late evenings while a group of local Garhwali priests chant sonorous hymns in praise of the Lord.

The Shrine is flanked on one side by ancient alleys wherefrom function the ubiquitous clan of the Panda's – the traditional facilitators of religious rituals and guarantors of the pilgrim's administrative well being against a modest 'dakshina' (donation), a friend, guide and philosopher in lands afar and difficult. On the other flank is the Tapt Kund (hot springs) where the devotees have a bath most refreshing. The attraction of hot bath against the bone-jarring cold regularly drew the troops from the small military garrison located in the 'Mana Camp' to this spot. Consigned to isolation and deprivations, that was an occasion of much joy and merriment for these troops.

Mana Camp

Just two kilometres Northwards of Badrinath Temple, upstream of River Alaknanda and on its the opposite bank is situated the village of Mana. Below the village, River Alaknanda takes a turn to the North-East towards its origin, the Alakapuri Glacier, eight kilometres uphill and at an altitude of 15,000 feet. A goat trail runs along, used by the Bhotias to take their cattle to graze upon the rich plants that spring to life after the snow cover recedes. It is believed that having completed their sojourn in this world, King Yudhishthira, wife Draupadi and the other four Pandavas had taken to this trail on their way to the Heaven. Mythology further states that all except the King himself had to discard their physical being to atone for the sin they might have committed, while only the King, guided by a dog, made it to the Heaven alive. Truly, burly and handsome local dogs still abound – they are the soldiers' darlings who when in rest, nestle cosy to give warmth against biting cold, and lead the way when moving on hazardous patrol duty.[6] As for the death of the four of the Pandavas and Draupadi's, it is quite understandable that anyone taking to that trail would be unlikely to survive for long.

Just as River Alaknanda turns North-West towards her origin, the legendry River Saraswati joins her coming down from its origin at the watershed of the Himalayan Range on the Indo-Tibet Border. River Saraswati originates at the eighteen thousand five hundred feet high Mana Pass, located 46 kilometres further North of Mana where the Indo-Tibet Border is delineated. From there it flows down Southwards till it hits the Mana George just short of Mana Village. The George is a narrow, deep slit in the mountain through which cascades the River Saraswati in accompaniment of a deafening roar and huge water spay. This is the four hundred feet drop of the Vasundhara Falls after which, at a confluence below the Mana Village, the river merges into River Alaknanda. That is where River Saraswati vanishes, never to reappear again, even if its existence in the ancient plains West of River Jamuna has been proven by the signs of her hydrographical remnants.

Situated astride this confluence, Mana village is a cluster of densely built stone-mud-mortar huts spread over a bowl shaped reverse slope. It is here that the nomadic Bhotia's migrate to every summer months to graze their yaks and sheep and carry on with the business of life, a bit of agriculture included.

Up ahead North of the village, the reverse slope ends in a steep climb. Halfway along that climb sits a huge boulder made of laminate-like layers of rock slabs, its overhang providing for a natural shelter, known as the Ved Gufa (cave). It is not difficult to imagine this boulder as a giant book, and so it is stated to be the site where Saint Veda Vyas composed the great epic of ancient times, the Mahabharata. Further up, a steep and narrow mule track led to the great Mana George.

Short of the village and located on either bank of River Alaknanda was the 'Mana Camp' of the Army, a logistic base to maintain the outposts

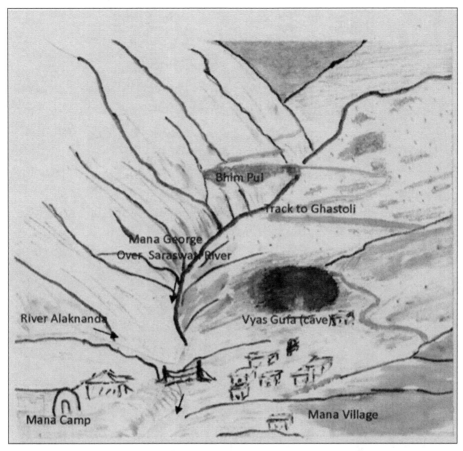

Mana Village

deployed yonder. These outposts had the onerous task of keeping watch over the 'Mana Pass' on the Indo-Tibet Border while living under conditions so extreme and deprived that today's better endowed soldiers would not be able to imagine. Mana Camp was a cluster of rudimentary shelters made of corrugated galvanised iron-sheets nailed to timber ballies (poles) and two Nissen Huts, and heated by few kerosene bukhari's.[7] It is near this camp that we pitched our snow tents to establish our own little base. Here we would hold our stores and equipment and from here we would reconnoitre the entire landscape as a part of the Gurkha battalion which was responsible for the defence of this sub-sector of the Joshimath Sector. And while we geared up for the series of reconnaissance patrols up to the Indo-Tibet Border, we would proceed at the slightest opportunity to bathe in the hot springs under the benevolent gaze of Lord Badrinath.

Soon we befriended the Rawal himself, a youngster in his mid-twenty's who had been selected to take the place of the recently demised head priest of the Temple, and who clearly longed for young company which only we could offer. It was an easy, open and joyous friendship between a strictly bound religious head and a group of earthy soldiers mandated into equally severe but yet more rigorous living. Of course, the get-togethers had no religious or tactical agenda; song, story and supper prevailed. The Lord's influence turned many amongst my troops to vegetarian diet; the regulation two pegs of rum, of course, being retained as a harmless part of that diet.

To the Great Himalayan Heights Yonder

A mule track took off from Mana Village to take to a steep up-gradient to a spot just above the sheer Mana George. Here it crossed over the George at its narrowest gap over a natural bridge of awesome design. Over the thirty feet odd gap between the two opposite shoulders of the George is a neatly placed and perfectly chiselled giant rock, its levelled top providing for a safe passage across. This is the Bheem Pul (bridge); legend says that the massive rock was shaped and placed by Bheem, the most powerful prince among the five Pandava brothers. Indeed, looking at the bridge from afar it is a wonderful sight of natural engineering even if a sceptic observer is not prepared to grant to Bheem his ingenuity.

It was here, on a rocky outcrop short of the Bheem Pul, that our Patrol Leader, a tall tough and handsome Major from the Gurkha Battalion, decided to site the patrol rendezvous. Earlier the battalion commander's briefing was held at the battalion headquarters – a cluster of rudimentary bunkers located on the reverse slope of a high feature that dominated the valley ahead. A day later, the Patrol Leader briefed the entire patrol consisting of a platoon of new Gorkha recruits and my section of sappers. I took among my sappers, two hailing from the local Bhotia community and two from the Garhwal region.

I also decide to take my two dogs along. 'Mohan' was a huge, strong, black and hairy local Bhotia canine who was already an adult when he decided to adopt our camp as its resident mascot. He was humourless, a serious fellow who took his responsibility of supervising the camp very diligently – a sort of silent well wisher. 'Bhutto' was a prancing pup who offered his companionship by following me when I was once coming down from my platoon post at the call of our headquarters. As I passed by a small, remote settlement, a lady demanded that I accept the pup's offer; in return for the consultancy, she promised to relieve my platoon of a sack of rice. As we shall see later, company of these two characters helped.

The task of the patrol was spelt out: one, to evaluate various tactical parameters of the terrain between Mana and the Border; and two, to mark our presence at the exact point where the highest watershed in the sector lies and which demarcates the natural alignment of the Indo-Tibet Border. As the task involved carrying out reconnaissance along the many gullies and high grounds on either side of the Saraswati Valley besides the main valley itself, it was to be a sixteen day self-contained patrol. In fact, if the rules of acclimatisation were to be followed, the patrol would have had to halt for four days after every three thousand feet of climb, and that would have stretched the duration of the patrol to more than twenty days. That was too long a time to be 'self-contained', which meant that one carried, besides one's arms, ammunition, equipment and 'extreme cold climate clothing', his food, fuel, sleeping bag and his share of the centralised stores.[8] The Patrol Leader therefore decided to ignore the rules of acclimatisation and decreed that the patrol would march double the usual distance daily, thus limiting the duration to just twelve days. Cutting short the duration thus was welcomed by all of us.

Off to a Long Range Patrol

Summer was approaching and that meant that the Sun rays would cause the snow where it lay over rocky patches to melt down; the same patches would be covered with slippery frost once the Sun made his exit or moved behind the tall peaks. During the first half of the day, clear, dust free sky allowed the Sun rays to remain intense enough to burn exposed human skin, and aided by reflected radiation from the snow all around, cause what is known as 'snow burn'. At its best it causes blackened faces and skin peeling off from cheeks, nose, ears and fingers; at its worst it causes swelling, reddening and intense pain.[9] Usually in these heights, by the mid-day, clouds would coalesce from the ambient moisture to blank out the Sun rays and that would bring the temperatures down to below the freezing point.

It was on such a clear sunny day when we assembled short of the Bheem Pul and had our final briefing, inspection, tea and the customary 'hurrah'. The first destination was the post of Ghastoli and the march as well as the reconnaissance was to be conducted over the next two days. Each carrying over thirty five kilogramme of load, we set off at 7.30 A.M. The temperature was minus five degrees and a cold sharp wind whizzed past the single file of marching troops.

We crossed over Bheem Pul to take to the mule track running along the right bank of the Saraswati Valley. The beginning was scary. It was a four feet wide mule track that was cut into sheer vertical rock – it was like a sky walk three hundred feet or so over the fast flowing River Saraswati. Marching over that stretch while carrying large loads and weapons was hazardous to state the least, particularly when the clearance was further constricted by rocky overhangs and sharp turns. Once through, we picked up speed over a gradual up-slope taking ten minutes break every two hours or so. At noon, there was a half-hour break when we lunched on thick sweetened 'puri', rendered rock hard by cold, and dry egg and potato mix 'subji', all washed down with a kind of scalding hot beverage which went by the nomenclature of 'chai'. I utilised these breaks to note down my observations and rough measurements, and to list out the photographs taken.

In the days of yore, this mule track was a trade route over which caravans of local ponies, laden with goods to be bartered between the Indian traders and their Tibetan counterparts, plied every summer month.

Starting from the month of May every year, the State Public Works Department undertook to repair the nature's damages caused to the track during the winter. This was done by manually arranging locally collected stones of various sizes and shapes to level the surface and topping it up with rammed earth. The task was assigned to more or less hereditary contractors from Joshimath and Mana. The track had also to run over many crossings across streams that run down from the hill sides to join the River Saraswati. These crossings were made of timber logs felled across the gaps or boulders arranged in the manner of dry masonry. Repair of these crude crossings was also undertaken by the State. At the time of our patrol, repairs had just about commenced, but even otherwise, we found the track surface in a reasonably good condition. Crossings over the fast and furious streams over the contraption that went by the description of 'bridge' was another matter though – it was a venture which filled one with many doubts.

The Patrol Routine

On the first day itself we set out a routine for ourselves. Rising at dawn after a night long state of extreme cold and weariness induced stupor that passed off as 'sleep', we would 'go around the boulders' and then to any of the nearby streams to wash and brush; the running water was cool, not cold, and refreshing. Of course, the Havildar Major would have earmarked separate boulders and streams for the officers – the two of us, the Patrol Leader and his Deputy – and the men. Meanwhile, men detailed for the purpose would light up a makeshift fire to prepare a breakfast of 'puri-sabji-chai' which the patrol would partake in unbelievable quantities while sitting in a close circle. Then, after a short briefing and discussion related to the day's task and administrative details, we would set off by about 7.30 A.M, halting after every two hours or so for a mug of quickly brewed tea. Besides, of course, there were halts whenever it was needed to engage in recording the attributes of the terrain.

A longer halt for lunch would be called by the Havildar Major at noon and then, just as the weather would turn extremely hostile after

3 P.M. or so, a night camp site would be selected on the bank of a stream. Some men would be sent out to collect dry brushwood and light a fire. Then the nominated soldiers would get busy preparing a 'hot meal' of rice, tinned mutton curry and tinned vegetables. As the patrol sat in a circle around the fire, there would be the much awaited event of 'rum issue' accompanied with song, dance and jokes. The dinner would be served before the 'last light' (dusk) while the 'cooks' of the day would get after preparing huge quantities of 'shakkar-para' and 'namak-para' that would be distributed to serve as emergency ration.[10] Thus having met all ends, we would spread our sleeping bags over a layer of rubberised 'ground sheet', get into it in full gear, and seal ourselves from the freezing cold, as much as we could, with a blanket thrown over the sleeping bag.[11] Mohan and Bhutto, however, were quite 'at home' with the cold, in fact energised by it. They slept on my either side, radiating some additional warmth to my shivering bones.

Ghastoli

The second day's march was an unforgettable experience. As we went up and down over the mule track below the tall peaks, we could see the River Saraswati flowing thousands of feet below us – it was a pleasant sight. The narrow river bed as well as the points where the tributary streams rushed down from heights on either bank to met it were strewn with rocks and boulders small and big, the bigger ones of the size of a two-bedroom flat. Erosion caused by thousands of years of Sun, wind and snow effects on the mountain wall on either side had caused these chunks of rock to develop cracks and then tumble down to rest on the river bed, sometimes even altering its course. Soon we were witness to this awesome event when the opposite bank of the river shook with the massive force and deafening sound of a huge boulder rolling down, bouncing like a ball and bringing down in its wake a massive train of moraine. We thanked our stars that the nature's play was enacted on the opposite side of the river.

Our first sighting of Ghurrals came on this day. These are mountain goats, tall and big but so amazingly nimble footed as to be able to jump from one rock to another over deep precipices in perfect balance and landing. There were five of them scattered over a patch of tough brushwood, apparently doing nothing else than watching us from various angles by turning their neck to, fro, up and down. A month earlier, egged on by our Brigade Ordnance Officer, a feudal Rajput from Rajasthan, I had shot one for the pot from a distance of over 800 metres and had to retrieve the hulk from a thousand feet deep gully. Obviously, that was my last such venture.

Two days march took us to a spot where graziers set up their tents to keep a watch over their herds of sheep. The spot was known as Ghastoli, situated at nearly fifteen thousand feet altitude. Short of this spot, one had to cross over to the left bank of the River Saraswati, the crossing helped by two rickety, creaking and swaying remnants of tree trunks which had been thrown across the rushing water below. This 'bridge' crossed, we landed up on a flat table land where stood a 'Nissen Hut' lived in by a detachment of the Army's Garhwal Scouts. It could accommodate only half our strength and so we put the younger lot inside. It was early for the graziers to turn up and so the rest of us ensconced ourselves within the mud-stone enclosures that were meant to keep the sheep after sundown. That evening the usual song-and-rum routine was observed with more verve. Then we slept; we had a long, lonely march ahead.

Morning brought us an awesome sight of the valley below. It was wide, nearly flat in the middle, and majestic in its white, brown, grey and black hues. I had some observations to record off the mule track and so took off early with my men, to join up some distance away with the rest of the patrol by 9 A.M. or so.

To Rattakona

The range of information data to be collected would increase as we moved more and more into the desolate areas. This day therefore, it was a long march with many more halts for close reconnaissance, till at about 4 P.M. when we come across a collapsed bridge; it was made of dry stone masonry and its crude arch had given away under the weight of snow-slide. We could have crossed over the snow-slide but the snow had melted with the rise in temperature. Fed by snow-melt over the entire day, the stream had heavy volume water gushing through it and the current was very strong. However, since the cold night would freeze the fury by the early part of the morning, so we decided to halt here for the night.

Next day was more or less a repeat of the previous one. Around mid-day we found the rock overhang under which a group of four constables of the Uttar Pradesh Provincial Armed Constabulary had perished about a month earlier.[12] They were returning from one of the border surveillance posts when they were caught by a snow blizzard. Ignorant of survival techniques under such situations, they has taken shelter under this overhang and settled down around a fire – only one escaped freezing to death. A helicopter could be arranged only after three days to retrieve the lone survivor, the dead were brought back many days later. Being the first ones to be there after the mishap, we cleared the left over food, cigarette packets etc. that lay strewn about and raised a stone cairn to commemorate the departed braves.

At the end of the day's march we had entered such high altitude that the ground was rugged no more. It had opened out of the claustrophobic mountain walls and turned more like a plateau, heights on either flank being just about few hundred feet higher. Of course, the mountains and the glaciers beyond the valley and its numerous gullies remained formidable to the extreme, mind boggling it their vast expanse, covered with snow and dotted with black patches where rock had shrug free of its white blanket. Breathing was strenuous, feet seemed heavy and shoulders became so numb that we did not feel the heavy load any more – thankfully. Strong winds, carrying specks of snow that struck our face like pin-pricks was an added irritant.

The weather chose to 'pack up', which meant that calling off the march would favour preservation of life, and so we decided to halt early and set up our camp for the night. For the camp, I found a scenic natural amphitheatre surrounded by small mounds that kept the wind out. Then every matter attended to, I found good time to jot down my observations in much details. In the early part of the night. a short snow blizzard found us huddling closer for mutual protection, but thankfully it passed by after an hour or so; I was better off with Mohan and Bhutto by my side. In the later half of the night a clear sky opened up for us to gaze upon the majestic moon-lit landscape. It was divine.

The fifth day's march was uneventful. At about 3 P.M. we reached the Rattakona Camp, situated at an altitude of nearly 17,000 feet. It was a semi-permanent summer camp of the Special Police Force which was occupied by a platoon of the constabulary from March to November every year. Even during the winters, when the land access became impassable, few men would be left to keep a watch, living on tinned food and composite rations. Only those who have been through such situations for a length of time would appreciate the situation, and the grit and determination that is needed to live through it.

There was one Nissen Hut meant for the visiting patrols. A newly promoted Deputy Superintendent of Police, a tough but grumpy character welcomed us and we settled down to savour the little luxuries that materialised – bukhari heaters, hot water bathing space, 'bore-hole' toilet, sleeping bunks, hot half-cooked food and news and song from a 'transistor' radio.[13] Sight of a volleyball court of sorts made us happy in anticipation of some fun the next day which was set aside as an 'administration day'. The policemen were happy too, having some new company to enliven their drab lives.

By the late evening our host had imbibed enough rum, even if it is extremely harmful to do so in such heights. He then turned aggressive while contending that we were indeed his 'guests', and so we had no business to join in the camp's administrative chores, and that he would not be denied his right to attend to us even if we were a 'bunch of aggressive, fearless and arrogant soldiers' (sic). While that drama was going on, I worked on my observations. I had a fitful sleep, filled in with the usual high altitude hallucinations and heavy breathing; frequent swigs of water helped.

The entire day next was spent on changing clothes, washing these, reading a novel, writing my notes and participating in a game of volleyball, a game that I somehow never got to like. The troops had good rest, even if many of the new recruits complained of altitude induced headache. Some Aspirin and Vitamin C tablets cured them. By the way, it was my belief – that I find strange today – that these tablets contained nothing of medicinal value and the reliving effect on simpleton soldiers was merely psychological. However, as long as relief was brought about, I had no reason to complain.

The Mana Pass

In the afternoon, I and my buddy went out a few kilometres along the route that we would traverse to reach Mana Pass. There was no sign of the old pony track, unused as it was since the late 1950's. Soon we found a stream that had to be crossed. Snow-melt had made the steam un-fordable and so we decided to start very early the next day.

We started at 4 A.M. The gradient was gentle but the oxygen deficient high altitude made our progress tedious. Thankfully, since we planned to return before night fall, we carried only our small haversack and personal weapons. We used a safety rope to wade across the stream which was in spate even in the early morning. The Saraswati Valley here was a wide flat expanse, flanked by heights covered by snow. Massive glaciers rested in the bowls and gullies created by the heights and ridges around and the sight was awesome. As we came abreast the Tara Glacier, we halted for breakfast.

By 9 A.M. guided by the remnants of old halting spots, we reached a narrow ledge where started the last steep climb on the way to the Pass. It took us an hour to negotiate the climb during which, way below, I could recognise a residual lake-bed. This was the Ragas Tal (lake). According to the legend, this lake was dug by the 'Rakshas' (barbarian) clan to drink water from while they and the 'Dev' (God) clan joined hands to churn the ocean in their quest to find 'amrit' (elixir of immorality). There were sign of one bank of the lake having collapsed to

Rakshasha Taal (18000 feet) is on right foreground, trail to Mana Pass is seen on left foreground

Origin of River Saraswati as viewed from Mana Pass towards India. Deo Taal is seen on the middle ground

Deo Taal (18500 feet)

Last Stretch to Mana Pass (19600 feet)

Tibet as Viewed from Mana Pass

cause a massive land-slide and enormous volume of water to run out. May be that was the cause of a devastating flood in the River Alaknanda in 1970. My Bhotia sapper told me that having served the despicable Rakshas, that was the fate ordained for the Ragas Tal. I was sceptical; it was the Dev clan who cheated the Rakshas clan when the amrit was found, doing a vanishing trick with the pot of elixir. Shouldn't the lake which served the Dev clan have been paying for the breach of trust?

Indeed, just as we cleared the climb to march along a gradual up-slope, we were dazzled by a scene of heavenly beauty. It was an enormous lake of stark blue water, serene and calm save the ripples over its surface caused by a brisk wind. That was the Dev Tal, a lake dug by the Deva clan to quench their thirst during the vigorous churning of the ocean. We went down a gentle slope to its edge to dip our hands into the water enchanted by the soft sound of tiny ripples lapping the stone covered shore. We felt rewarded.

The joy was short lived when we noticed many of the young recruits struck by high-altitude nausea and headache. To their credit they ignored the exertion and moved on. The Nursing Assistant gave them Aspirin tablets – that is all that one could do. Soon we reached the 18,300 feet high Mana Pass. We had a tea and shakarpara halt for about an hour during which I went across the Pass. It was like standing on top of an amphitheatre as the Tibetan plateau, with its smoothly rounded and barren hills coloured in shades of white, brown and black, spread before. I tried to visualise as to where the closest Tibetan township of Tholingmath would be and the alignment of the route that led to it.

Unlike usual passes, Mana Pass was actually a slope running down a mountain range by moving along which it was easier to cross over to the other side of the watershed. The slope was steep as well as Sun facing and therefore it was mostly free of deep accumulation of snow. The point from where the old trail started its descent into Tibet was marked by a stone cairn. Just across, the slope turned into a near vertical wall that must have been caused by a land slide, practically blocking further move. A few metres to the East, across the border alignment, lay the North slope of the Balbala Glacier – an endless expanse of pure white snow.

Just a hundred metres short of the Pass, with drops of water from snow-melt trickling into a thin channel, rises the River Saraswati. Under a strange notion that someday I will tell my folks that I could cross the River in just one stride, I took a leap across. My 21 years old heart was delighted at this feat!

Then we turned back, reaching the Rattakona Camp just as it was getting dark at 8 P.M. After a day's break, we made it to the Pass once again.

A Long Trudge Back

On the eleventh day, the patrol started on its way back. Half the patrol was suffering from effects of high altitude and therefore we distributed their loads among us, the patrol leader and myself included. With the rations mostly consumed, the load was not exactly the double, but it was

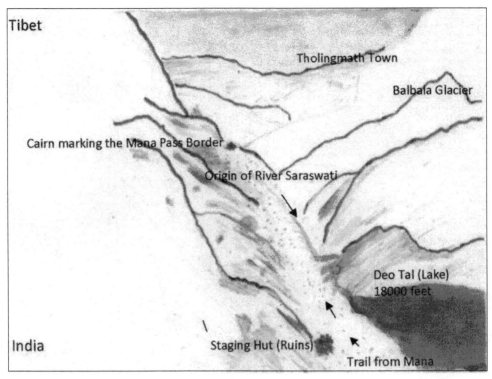

Tibet

Tholingmath Town

Balbala Glacier

Cairn marking the Mana Pass Border

Origin of River Saraswati

Deo Tal (Lake)
18000 feet

India

Staging Hut (Ruins)

Trail from Mana

Mana Pass (19600 feet)

the second sleeping bag and the rifle that I found to be a nuisance, a pain in fact – literally so.

We decided to cut the agony and marched the entire distance to Ghastoli in one day. All this time I remained occupied in confirming the observations made on our way up. Next day, a pleasant surprise came in the form of a platoon of Gurkhas that had arrived the previous day from Mana Camp. The Commanding Officer, a stern and forbidding personality, had sent the platoon to share our loads. Next day, I was off to Joshimath to be debriefed at the formation headquarters.

Twenty five years later I had an opportunity to fly in a helicopter over the entire route, and more. Nothing seems to have changed. Nature has its own long, very long time table.

NOTES

1. Such patrolling to keep the border under surveillance is a routine except during the winter months when the areas contiguous to the border are rendered impassable due to heavy snow cover.

2. Starting from Rishikesh, first came Dev Prayag, where Rivers Bhagirathi and Alaknanda joined to form River Ganga. Then came Rudra Prayag followed by Karna Prayag where Rivers Mandakini and Pindar merged with River Alaknanda flowing down from Badrinath via Joshimath where River Dhauli Ganga joined her at Vishnu Prayag.

3. When the temple remains closed from the month of November till June due to heavy snow, Lord Badrinath is worshiped here in His Narasimha Avatar (incarnation). This Math then becomes the Lord's winter abode.

4. True to their habit, in this sector too, the Chinese claim one part of our territory, the 'Barahoti Plains' and some pockets that would make the border alignment suit their predatory instincts. In the days gone by, the Barahoti Plains hosted a major annual fair where apart from religious rituals, the Tibetans and the Indian Bhotia clan traded wool, silk, salt, etc. China's belligerence has disrupted that tradition, as indeed it was intended by the Communist regime.

5. Auli was Army's training area; it had a firing range used by the soldiers as well as the policemen of the Indo Tibet Border Police. The rest of the meadow was a beautiful landscape, its gentle slopes covered in the winters with a smooth blanket of snow. While a modern training area functions, today it is also a tourist destination and a popular destination for snow skiing.

6. Local dogs are of immense value to the troops. Besides offering friendship and entertaining antics, they could warn the soldiers of the danger from crevasses, avalanches and land slides. My platoon had one, a huge fellow called 'Mohan' who was strong enough to carry a man's load during long marches. Then I had 'Bhutto', a pup who chose to adopt me.

7. These huts were of First World War vintage, designed in 1916 by Major Peter Nissen of the Royal Engineers, and very sturdy, in the shape of horizontal half cylinder, and housing within it sleeping bunks and kerosene bukharis (heaters). These were moved man or mule pack in dismantled state and constructed in-situ. Ingenuous soldiers improved it further against extreme cold by lining the canopy from inside with old blankets.

8. Today's soldiers may not be aware that the weapons, ammunition and all other items of necessary accoutrements weighted nearly forty percent more that what they have to carry these days. The system of porters and ponies was rarely sanctioned and for provision for helicopter resupply one needed to stretch his imagination to the level of fantasy.

9. There was no snow clothing those days, only what was known as the 'Extreme Cold Climate Clothing' – an effective but heavy version of today's snow clothing, and much inferior to today's 'special clothing'. There was no 'Vaseline' issue to protect against 'snow burn', the purpose was solved by frequent rubbing of mustard oil over exposed skin.

10. These are dry fried sweetened or salty biscuit-like snack made of flour and butter. Actually, however, despite my orders that the emergency ration would be consumed only on my permission, troops quietly munched away the day's issue within an hour or two of the start of the march; I looked the other way.

11. We wore khaki serge trousers over white colour semi-woollen under-pants (known as 'long johns'), similar vests under 'Angola Shirts' brown in colour, then an olive green jersey, and finally a long jacket of green colour. Stockings were made of khaki twine which, being hazardous to the feet, had to be worn over standard issue socks which helped in keeping the freeze out. For boots, we preferred the 'jungle boots' against the 'snow boots' which was comfortable only when one did not have to move.

12. In those days, the UP-Tibet Border was guarded by a Special Police Force of the UP State's Provincial Armed Constabulary. The unit was manned by tall, handsome and tough men coming from the high caste Awadhi people for whom the British had much respect, their participation in the 1857 Revolt notwithstanding. The Force had posts established close to the UP-Tibet Border, living in Nissen Huts, surviving on composite rations and leading a life difficult. Later Indo-Tibet Border Police took up that responsibility. Life in such posts, tough though, is more liveable these days.

13. Bore hole was a nine inch diameter hole bored into the ground with help of an earth auger. The excavated earth was piled up next to it and a shovel was left there. Covered with tent, tarpaulin, corrugated sheet or hessian cloth depending on the resources at hand, it served as officer's toilet. For men, there were 'shallow' or 'deep trench' latrines depending on the period of use, the trench covered by a timber platform and a Kanat (cloth screen) strung all around. These latrines were sited some distance away, a yellow flag warning unsuspecting intruders of the impending consequences. Much later, in Sri Lanka, I had my company's 'wash rooms' – as these are referred to these days – sited, yellow flag and all, to cover one of the enemy's approaches. It seemed to have worked !

*

3

'War' of the Junkyard

The story is set in the early 1970's, somewhere close to the Indo-Tibet Border in what was known then as the 'North-East Frontier Agency', now the state of Arunachal Pradesh. The place was devoid of human inhabitation. Obviously it did not have the distinction of having a name, and was therefore referred to as the 'Y-Junction' in Army's parlance. Across a terrain most hazardous, soldiers had cut a rough track to this location and set up a brigade headquarters there. The honour of being named as a 'junction' was justified by three mule tracks which took off Northwards from this location towards the border passes at heights ranging from 15,000 to 18,000 feet. These tracks were the logistic life-lines to maintain three infantry battalions and some support troops that were tasked to defend this part of the McMahon Line.

Chinese troops positioned across the passes had not exactly been friendly. Since their aggression in 1962, they had been carrying on with their inimical gestures, dispensing 'warnings' in 1965 and again in 1971 against some imaginary 'threats' posed by the Indians of which the Indians themselves were unaware, but actually to assure Pakistan of their all-weather solidarity. The situation called upon the Army to prepare fortifications to defend the McMahon Line, and that brought the

Y-Junction to a prominence that it was denied so far. Hundreds of tonnes of material for construction of defence works was transported from the foothills and dumped here before being broken into smaller mule-pack loads and moved Northwards. Thus over the years, Y-Junction had accumulated large heaps of unusable, leftover and salvaged junk of metals, timber, stone etc. strewn all over, wherever there was some flattish space was to be found. The sight, no doubt, was not pleasant to military eyes accustomed as they are to order and from.

"This junkyard is a bloody eyesore!", thundered the recently posted brigade commander. The gentleman was famous for his massive moustache', physical courage and rude manners. "Have these cleared out, pronto!", he barked at his Brigade Major. As the principal staff officer of the brigade headquarters, it was the young Major's burden to suffer his commander, a role he bravely performed with much cheer and little visible despondency.

> "We did try once before, Sir, but the cost of removing the mountain of load is much more than its salvage value. Therefore, no one at the 'base' is prepared to accept this headache", confided the Brigade Major,

> "Then have these thrown down the precipice into any of the gorges around here", shot back the Commander, a bit irritated at having been replied to, "I do not want to see this garbage",

> "Sir, where will we find manpower to do so? Infantry and engineers are up preparing defences, artillery is clearing their deployment areas, signals are running around to keep the communications going ..., no troops are available, nor is there any civilian population to hire labour from. I do not know how can we clear out this junk-mountain", lamented the Brigade Major. He was not about to give up to a bully,

> "I do not like to hear excuses, Major. I shall be back from my forward area reconnaissance in a week's time. I do not wish to set my eyes upon this garbage when I return", the Commander concluded the matter, settling into his sphinx-like countenance.

A week later, the Commander returned; he found Y-Junction clean in its pristine glory. For the 'nth' time he smugly congratulated himself on his habit of enforcing his conviction even if he could see the impracticability of his order; he knew that to be the hallmark of the 'great captains' of all times. Actually, he expected the Brigade Major to tell him about the 'power of his inspiration' and the latter's 'resolve to implement the impossible'. But even as days passed, he found the Brigade Major's silence on the matter a bit strange. "Subordinates usually come up instantly to report completion of such uphill assignments and claim the credit for it", he mused. A week later, with the Brigade Major still not obliging, the curiosity got better of his stony demeanour.

> "Young fellow, I see you have had the junk cleared, that too on time. I am glad", he announced when he could no longer contain his urge to know as to how was this work accomplished,
>
> "Yes Sir", murmured the Brigade Major before changing the topic,
>
> "Well, how did you do it?", the Commander's iron curtain seem to be melting, much to his annoyance in succumbing to such instinctive curiosity,
>
> "I could not find any one to give the job to. So when Second Lieutenant X came down to attend to some chore, I instructed him to take on this task",
>
> "Who is this fellow X?",
>
> "He is the engineer platoon commander at 'Z-La', he has gone back to his platoon",
>
> "Hmm!, let me see him the next time he is around", ruled the Commander.

The scene now shifts to the Commander's office-hut, "tiger's den" so to say. The worthy 'Tiger' was sprawled resplendent on his throne-like chair while the Brigade Major and Second Lieutenant X stood in attention.

After making them wait for a regulation five minutes that was meant to build up anxiety in his subordinates, the Commander looked up. Focusing at infinity, he enquired of no one in particular, "What was done to clean up the junkyard?",

> On a cue from the Brigade Major, the Lieutenant replied, "Sir, I called that *Sardarji* (a Sikh gentleman) who comes to deliver

engineer stores and asked him to take away all the junk in his returning transport. He was very ... er... cooperative",

"Hmmm ..., I am sure you have done the required paper work", he looked at the Brigade Major; the Lieutenant was too lowly for him to look at. "These were government property and must be disposed of according to proper procedure even if these have to be buried or thrown. If you haven't, do so now",

"The junk could not have been cleared if we followed the rules, Sir. Had it been practical to do so, it would have been done long ago, don't you think so?", this was the stupid 21 years old Second Lieutenant, innocent of the height, might and wrath of a Brigadier. The stunned silence at a Lieutenant's audacity in uttering words before the brigade commander was palpable,

"Hmmmm ....",

"Sir, actually, I sold off the junk. It fetched three thousand two hundred and fifty rupees. The cash has been deposited with the Camp Commandant", the Lieutenant seemed unable to keep his mouth shut,

Silence ..., and then hell broke loose!

"You did what!", the Commander jumped out of his chair, nearly so. "You sold off government property, you fool!! How could you commit such an offence?"..... He looked right, left, above and below, drummed the table with his fingers and threw his hands up, when the Lieutenant lost patience and interrupted the proceedings,

"But Sir, the headquarters got three thousand two hundred and fifty rupees! It can fund ten *Barakhana's* (soldier's community feast), Sir!",

"This fellow is mad!, remove him from my presence ..... at once!", the Commander was shouting now. "He will send all of us to jail, this idiot!!".

The intrepid Lieutenant was about to open his mouth again when the Brigade Major turned and asked him to follow. Once in his office, he let the Lieutenant have it, "I like your *josh*. I also suspected that you were a moron. That suspicion has come true! Bloody fool, who asked you to tell the whole story to the Commander? Now get out, vanish! I have had enough of you. Do not be seen till further orders. Go up to your platoon, let your troops suffer you!",

"Are you angry with me, Sir?", the Lieutenant asked innocently,

"Oh, no, how could I be, in fact I admire you! I was a damn fool to have given you this task", annoyance was apparent in the Brigade Majors voice. At this stage, the conversation was interrupted by Commander's summons to the Brigade Major, who departed to face what would invariably be another bout of 'tiger's' wrath, but not before throwing to the Lieutenant a hard stare and a dismissive swipe of hand, of the kind one applies to shoo away a crow.

The Commander was still in a state of rage. He was also concerned about the fate of the young Lieutenant who could face punishment for 'misappropriation' of public property. Being conscious that allowing such a fate to befall a budding leader of men would be considered as a slur on any superior officer's professionalism and character, he understood, much contrary to his instincts, that calm rather than anger was needed to manage this complex situation.

"Were you aware of … er … the sale of the junk?", the Commander asked,

"I gave him full authority to do whatever he could to be rid of the junk. I also endorsed his action when he came to deposit the cash",

"Was it the right thing for X to do?',

"Yes Sir, though he went a bit too far when he took the Sardarji to be thrown down the precipice and so forced him to buy the junk at a price that the Sardarji says will sink his business. Of course, the slimy fellow is exaggerating",

"You endorse this illegal act!, Strange! Whose service are you in, the Army's or that fellow X's?", the tone was belligerent now,

"X's"… It is not known if it was an inadvertent slip of tongue or a misunderstanding of the query, but the reply caused the Commander to go into a state of uncontrolled rage,

"God!, what kind of men have you surrounded me with? Get them out of my hair or else I will shoot them!". The Commander, as if he was repeating a cycle of exercise, stood up, raised both his hands, clenched his fists, brought them down to his chest level; that was probably his manner of expressing exasperation. He repeated the rigmarole over and over again,

"The brigade's reputation is ruined! Report the matter to the divisional headquarters. We are finished!", the last remark was directed at the Brigade Major.

Matters moved fast hereafter. The Brigade Major confided with the Commanding Officer of the Lieutenant, who, in a moment of 'happy mood', narrated the episode to the top commander, 'God' so to say, the General Officer Commanding.

During the customary evening chat between commanders, the General Officer Commanding congratulated the Brigade Commander, "Well done old boy. You got rid of that junk yard which no one else could all these years. Every time I saw it, my mercury went up. Thank God, and thank you!",

"Thank you, Sir, it was very kind of you to have noticed this small development", murmured the confused Commander,

"Considering the cost of lugging the junk-load to the scrap market, it was quite a profitable transaction for the state exchequer. In the bargain we got rid of the eye-sore", the boss was ecstatic. "Add another thousand from me and give your troops a good *Barakhana*. God bless you".

The matter ended thus.

*

4

What Price, Saitan Singh?

The winding, wide and flat valley stretches far, as far as one can see, flanked by rolling mountains, seventeen to twenty thousand feet high. It is brown and white all over, the colour of gravel and weather-shattered pieces of rock interrupted by patches of snow. As the hard labour to reach this desolate high altitude desert comes to fruition, biting cold needles into your tired bones and massive gusts of roaring, freezing wind plays havoc with whatever is left of you. The immensity of listless desolation bluntly confirms what we all know; that man is a dwarf, of no consequence, a hapless toy of nature. Yet, there is life in here. Wild ass, king size raven and striped chameleon patterned in grey and white roam nonchalantly, nibbling at the tough desert grass and a variety of insects who emerge from nowhere to sustain the eternal cycle of life.

The Chushul Valley. The base of the Magger Hill is seen to the left.

Leaving the tiny hamlet of *Chushul* behind, the dirt track takes you past the abandoned air field, once a hub of hectic activity and now waiting dispassionately for a second coming. And then, suddenly, you come upon a simple cement-marble memorial that stands serenely amongst the wild asses, the ravens and the chameleons, blending perfectly into the mountainous surroundings as if it was a natural part of it. In a way it is, for it commemorates those one hundred and eight soldiers who chose to

The old Memorial

lie here forever. There sits this memorial, at the base of the crocodile shaped *Maggar Hill*, a part of the feature that the officers and men of a rifle company of the 13th Battalion of the Kumaon Regiment died defending.

The epitaph moves even the die-hard skeptic:

> *How can a man die better,*
>   *than facing fearful odds;*
> *For the ashes of his fathers,*
>   *and the temples of his Gods. (Macaulay)*

As the cold October of 1962 inched ominously towards an even colder November, the men of C Company, 13 KUMAON, prepared for the inevitable Chinese attack on *Rezang La*, a seventeen thousand feet plus tactically important pass which the Chinese wanted very badly. "You will defend Razang La", Major Saitan Singh was instructed by his Commanding Officer only a week earlier. Since then it had been a back-breaking effort. Bunkers and fortifications had to be constructed from materials lugged up laboriously over the oxygen depleted mountains over hours-on-end. There was little wherewithal available anyway and all that the 38 year old Major could hope for was a few crude bunkers and trenches which would give him a marginally better chance to put up a better fight. There was little food and even less water. Cotton uniform, semi-woollen pullover, thin, coarse blanket and a pair of hobnailed leather boots – meant to be used in plains – was all that these men had to beat the cold at minus fifteen degrees Celsius. Indeed, they also had some vintage 'great-coats' too, to be rotated amongst the night-duty personnel. But known problems can always be tackled. What the *Kumaonis* did not know was that they deserved better than the vintage bolt action rifles, unreliable machine guns and inaccurate mortars. They also deserved more ammunition, mines and artillery support so that they could live a little longer and prolong the nation's struggle against an invader. Yet, the available records and dispatches lead to very remarkable observations regarding these braves: first, withdrawal or surrender once the position became untenable – a wise military practice – was never even considered as an option; second, ill prepared and ill equipped as they were, there was no rancour amongst the men; and lastly, they were stoic about their impending fate. *Izzat* – of themselves, the unit and the motherland – was all that mattered. Death was not an issue.

The attack finally came on 18 October. Heavy artillery shelling pulverized the Kumaoni defences and then followed hordes of Chinese in one wave after the other. There wasn't enough weapons or ammunition to stop this torrent and as the Chinese closed-in, the Kumaonis jumped out of their trenches to engage them in vicious hand-to-hand combat with bayonets and rifle butts. Not having bargained for this kind of treatment, the Chinese broke rank and fled leaving their dead and dying behind. The *Ahirs* (soldiers of the cowboy class) of C Company, 13 KUMAON danced in joy, even as they knew that it was only a prelude to more ominous developments to come.

Soon the attack was renewed from a different direction. Shelling this time surpassed in intensity all previous attacks laying the modest Kumaoni defences wrecked and smouldering. But as the Chinese closed in, the silent trenches sprang to life again with the wounded and the dying putting up another display of stubborn fight. Surprised and shaken, the Chinese fled once again – those who could.

Depleted, weak and with little ammunition left, the Company was now attacked from the rear. Surrounded and with only a few left to continue the fight, the wounded Major repositioned his machine guns and prepared for the ultimate sacrifice. Finally, as the snowflakes drifted onto the surroundings and the day light faded away, the moment of reckoning arrived. The Major fell, having taken a full machine gun burst on his abdomen. So did his last companion, Company Havildar Major Harphul Singh. A new saga of supreme sacrifice and heroism had been written ; so pure, so devoid of any material considerations, that the hep 'gen-next' would find it unreal, unbelievable.

Razang La had fallen. So had the *Gurung Hill*, the *Goswami Hill* and *Sirijap Posts*, after the men defending these had fought till the last. Chushul and its great valley now lay ahead, weak and vulnerable, just for

World's one of the Largest Lakes, the Pangong Tso

the taking by the Chinese war machine. Yet, the Chinese did not move up any further. That is not so baffling if you consider that they might have had enough. They had bitten into steel and were now content in holding on to what they got. A bunch of 20-30 year old soldiers, led by a simple, duty-bound Major had embraced death defending an imaginary line drawn in Delhi's foreign office hundreds of kilometres away, while their age-group elsewhere cavorted in democratic freedom. What would have happened had they not chosen to do so ? Well, Chushul would be a foreign territory, Indian eyes wouldn't have savoured the awesome sight of the blue waters of Lake *Pangong Tso* and the wild asses would all have been eaten up, being rather agreeable to the Chinese palate.

But then, would it have made any difference ? Apparently none that touch our daily lives. Politicians would still be politicking on non–issues while amassing ill-gotten wealth, business world would yet be engaged in profiteering, the flower of the nation – the young – would still be fascinated by the yuppie, money making culture, and the rest of our countrymen

Wild Asses, the 'Kyangs', in Chushul Valley

would continue making a nuisance of themselves through goondaism, casteism, corruption and fights over language and religion. Yes, it would have made much difference to those one hundred and fourteen families. Their men would be leading well earned, comfortable retired life, the women wouldn't have had to bear through a life of constant struggles, shortages and anxieties, and the children wouldn't have had to grow up fatherless.

Like a son trying to un-see his father's deficiencies, the Memorial looks away from the Indian soil. Standing at the base of the feature those men died defending, it looks towards the land that was once ours, as if pleading for redemption. In 1994, the then Commanding Officer and his men, some of them sons of the fallen heroes, came to pay homage and installed a new marble milestone. It reads 'KM – O', signifying the beginning of a new journey.

Chushul is ours, so is Lake Pangong Tso. But was one hundred and eight lives a good price to pay for this ?

Yes, of course", would have insisted those Heroes.

Postscript

In Year 2012, the 'Battle of Rezang La' was commemorated on its Fiftieth Anniversary. The heroes were remembered and their martyrdom celebrated. In Gurgaon, a memorial was inaugurated by the Chief Minister. Some years earlier, the old Memorial at the Maggar Hill was expanded, beautified and consecrated.

*

5

On the Trail of the Dead: A Journey Through Karakoram

Preamble

Thanks to the *Siachen Glacier* and the Kargil War, most people are familiar with the region of *Ladakh* today. With the Kashmir Valley engulfed in militancy since the past two decades, the exotic landscape of Ladakh has also become a hot tourist destination – domestic as well as international. It is well that it is so, because there is no place in the Earth that unfolds before you the panorama of such an extraordinary landscape – vast, desolate, stark and cold, and yet beautiful in its mind-boggling hues of colours and contours.

Hidden behind those formidable mountain ranges are tales of unending human endeavour spread over thousands of years, to seek, to trade and to exchange ideas across natural barriers that leave little room for complacency in planning or undertaking journeys most hazardous. These are also the areas that saw the implementation of the catastrophic 'Forward Policy' adopted by the newly independent – and naïve – India in the late 1950's, in her innocent efforts to establish her control over the region of the *Aksai Chin*. China, meanwhile, had already occupied this area surreptitiously and built a road through it following her occupation of Tibet. As India raced to secure her boundary with a military force that was equipped with courage and little else, an unequal 'war' – if resistance unto death or incapacitation by a handful band of ill armed, ill equipped but dedicated soldiers may be termed thus – broke out. The slight of defeat haunts the psyche of every Indian to this day.

This is an account of a journey undertaken in the course of duty in the mid-1990 and in fulfillment of a long-standing desire to see the unseen. Notwithstanding the time lapse, it may be appreciated that even as the main township of *Leh* has changed much – what with a booming tourism industry and all round development in which the Army has made singular contributions – the outlying areas remains much the same today. The narration, therefore, remains valid.

A word about the 'ghosts' which find mention in the narrative. Modern, scientific outlook prohibits us from giving credence to these. However, besides providing some harmless amusement, it is also true that the locals firmly believe in the existence of these. Besides, 'ghosts' or 'spirits' find frequent mention even in the accounts of *Fa-hsien* and *Hsuan-tsang*, great men who had trodden over these lands in the early parts of the Christian Era. Inclusion of 'ghosts', therefore, may be in order; even the great scientist *Carl Segan* believed that human's knowledge is yet in its infancy and that there remains much unexplained by science.

The narration would be better understood if it starts with a glance over the map of the area – **Sketch 1**.

DAY 1: TO SASER BRANGSA

Saser La,[1] 5200 meters (17,100 feet)

1030 AM. The sight from atop the *Pass* was magnificent. I felt like a mountain goat standing high above the stark landscape. I filled my eyes with the incredible combination of different hues of brown, black, blue and ochre' that splashed majestically over the steep ridgelines of the *Karakoram Ranges* and the rugged valley of the *Shyok River* flowing 700 meters below from where I stood. "It is worth the tenuous climb", I

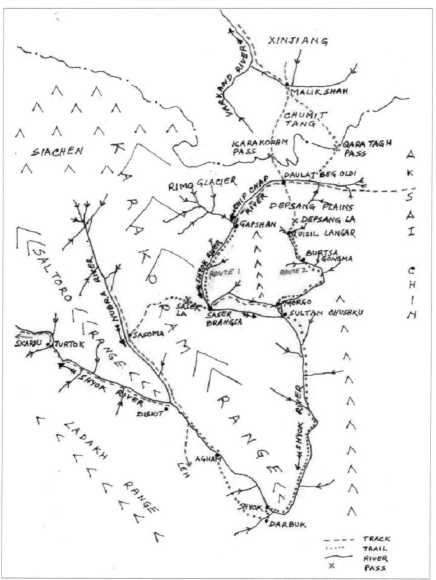

Sketch 1: A Rough Map of the Area Bounded by the Nubra and Shyok Valleys in Eastern Ladakh

mused as the cold, crisp mountain wind blew across my face.

We had started our climb at 0600 AM – self and my guide, *Tashi Norbu*. Tashi was a rifleman detailed to accompany me by the 'Ladakh Scouts' (a regiment of the local soldiers). He did not know how old he was, but was probably of my age, forty plus, who proved to be physically tougher than me – and that was a compliment not many would have been worthy of even in the Army. He never betrayed any emotion on his weather beaten, deeply lined countenance and yet took care of me in most innocuous ways. Over the next few days he became a companion and after the journey was over, we parted as friends, even as we knew that there was little chance of us meeting ever again.... But let us stick to the main narrative.

Sasoma, 3600 meters (11,800 feet)

Sasoma is a patch of flat stony ground on the Eastern Bank of *River Nubra* that emerges from the most formidable testing ground of soldiering that the Siachen Glacier undoubtedly is.

In the days of yore, it was a camping ground for the merchants who came from Northern Afghanistan, Gilgit, Hunza and Skardu, carrying their merchandise for trade at Yarkand and Kashgar in the province of Western Xingjian of China. No one can venture to guess as to when did the tradition of this arduous journey of over thousand kilometres across the most inhospitable territory in the world had started; it was there when the great travelers *Hsuan-tsang*, and *Fa-hsien* before him, had travelled across to India during the Seventh and Fourth Centuries of the Christian Era. Since Buddhism spread outwards from India, it is certain that the trail from Afghanistan and the North West Frontiers of ancient India, that headed across the *Saser La* and the *Karakoram Pass* towards Kashgar and beyond, was in use even before the beginning of the Christian Era.[2]

Presently, *Sasoma* was a cluster of mud huts which sheltered a detachment from the Border Roads Organisation. It was in one of those sparsely furnished yet very comfortable huts that I spent my night before the journey. We were up at 0430 A.M. and set off at 0600 A.M. for *Saser La* after a breakfast of puri, butter, jam and tinned fruit juice; high calorie intake was essential to survive at such altitudes, more so because loss of appetite was a common problem.

Saser La looms right above *Sasoma*, literally so, sitting 1600 meters above atop a craggy mountain wall which is nearly 70 degrees steep. The old trade caravan track was aligned astride the steep, snow fed seasonal nullah beds which run down from the ridgeline, and was presently virtually unusable. Some time ago, a motorable road had come up till half way to *Saser La*, the earth-boulder debris from its construction having obliterated the old track at many stretches. That, however, saved us from having to negotiate this steep climb loaded not unlike a mule, and a *Jonga*[3] dropped us off to trek the remaining ascent to *Saser La*. It took hard labour of a couple of hours to be there.

The pass, *Saser La,* was still covered with snow. We did not wait long there lest the body sweat froze inside our arctic clothing. The descent was equally steep besides being rather hazardous; snow and moraine had covered up the trail or what might have been left of it. Thus, by the early afternoon, we arrived at the next camping ground, *Saser Brangsa*, our halt for the night.

Saser Brangsa sits on the Eastern Bank of *River Shyok*, the river valley separating the *Karakoram Mountains* from the *Depsang Hills* to its East. There was a cable trolley erected by the Army Engineers to facilitate movement of loads across the River at this point. Like everywhere else in the desolate and harsh landscape of Ladakh, there was an enclosure made of stone-rubble that contained within its nook, some kerosene, dry twigs, matchboxes, dry fruit, some tinned food and fruit juices.[4] We halted here for the might, thinking of the rather long trek to *Gapshan* that lay ahead.

DAY 2: TO GAPSHAN

Saser Brangsa, 4500 meters (14,750 feet)

As one can see from Sketch 1, there were two routes from *Saser Brangsa* to *Karakoram Pass* and beyond to Xingjian in Tibet. **Route 1** ran Northwards upstream against the course of *River Shyok* upto *Gapshan*. Here terminates the *River Chip Chap*, flowing East to West from Aksai

Chin[5] in Tibet; it is actually a thin stream meandering over a wide and mostly dry nullah bed which joins up with *River Shyok* at the latter's point of origin.

From *Gapshan,* Route 1 ran upstream of the course of *River Chip Chap* up to *Daulat Beg Oldi.* **Route 2**, on the other hand, ran South-Eastwards from *Saser Brangsa,* following the downstream course of the same *River Shyok* upto *Sultan Chushku* and then turning due North via *Qizil Langar* and *Depsang La* to merge with Route 1 at *Daulat Beg Oldi.* We had decided to take Route 1 on our way out and return by Route 2.

The journey on Day 2 was uneventful. We moved astride the *River Shyok* along a pleasantly easy gradient, following a trail that was faintly distinguishable form the rest of the boulder strewn Shyok River Valley; there is something in human mind that can sense the imprint of his predecessor's intermittent footmarks made over thousand of years ago – a pleasant camaraderie between the present and its 'ghost'. You can not experience this benevolent bondage at Delhi or Chennai, or even at Guwahati or Kochi; you have to be in the lap of the all-powerful and majestic domain of the Nature, cold, breathless, helpless and vulnerable, to feel the 'spirits' goading you on. Over the cold, needle sharp wind lashing past an exhausted you, they whisper; "It will pass, do not give up", they say.

In a reversal of our vantage position at *Saser La,* we were now trudging along a deep valley, dwarfed by a steep rocky mountain wall on our right and a series of glaciers joining the River from our left. Occasionally we strained our necks to seek relief from a sense of being 'boxed–in' by looking at the narrow strip of blue sky that remained visible through the brown, black and white mountain walls. This was also the trail that was used by the few survivors of the attack on our post at *Daulat Beg Oldi* by the Chinese in October 1962. The valiant group of surviving infantrymen and engineers had destroyed what was left of their meager military hardware and supplies before withdrawing to *Thoise* over this same trail, wounded, cold and hungry. I felt a lump in my throat.

The Origin of Shyok River. Rimo Glacier is Seen in the Background

Somewhere halfway through our trek up North from *Saser Brangsa*, at a point up to which a vehicle could move astride the valley with some difficulty, we were met by a rather battered Jonga sent out from our post at *Gapshan*. Thus by the late evening we had reached *Gapshan* and secured ourselves inside a well insulated tent. After a meal of hard boiled rice, some half cooked 'lentil' – cooking is difficult in such rarefied atmosphere – and a piece of tinned vegetable, the menu rendered somewhat palatable by the addition of bottled pickle, we knocked off to rest our tired limbs and overworked lungs.

Shyok River, as one can see from Sketch 1, rises from the glaciated 'Rimo Group' of mountains at the Northern end of the massive *Karakoram Ranges*, somewhere near the North-most tip of our *Bharatvarsha*. The ruling altitude there is 6800 meters (22,500 feet) or so and wind blasts regularly at over 100 kilometres per hour, carrying miniscule specks of ice to pit painfully at your uncovered forehead and cheeks. The temperature fluctuates between minus 15 to minus 60 degrees Centigrade and there is wide variation between a sunny day when exposed skin burns dark brown and starts flaking, and after sunset when it becomes needle–cold within minutes. No living being can stay there unless one is an Indian Army man, though I am told that bacterial life forms may be found even in such regions.

This day, we were better off trudging along the valley floor. The sandy-gravel river bed was rather wide and covered with stones rounded to shape through eons of erosion by snow and water. Almost all stones were white in colour and that intrigued me; was it because these had been rubbing against snow for so long ? Then there are thin strips of blue water meandering within the mostly dry river bed and joined by numerous trickles of snow-melt water from either bank. The banks are strewn with various sizes of irregular shaped fragments of rocks which crack up due to the weathering action of wind and snow, and fall of endlessly from the mountain walls accompanied with sharp, thunderous noise. These rocks too are coloured in brown, but who could have ever known that there could be so many hues, shades and textures of this just one colour !

Erosion and weathering has made sure that the gradients along the valleys are gentle and the surface mostly unobtrusive. It was, therefore, not difficult to chart a path for passage of a vehicle or two, unless stopped by the intervention from a steep cutting or a gorge. Light and medium vehicles, para–dropped from military aircraft thus brought much relief to the troops – the Army men as well as the men of the Indo-Tibet Border Police (ITBP) – saving them from their excruciating drudgery through breathlessness and severe cold.[6] Today it saved us much time and energy.

DAY 3: TO DAULAT BEG OLDI

Gapshan, 4800 meters (15,750 feet)

An Air Force helicopter arrived at 0800 AM and hovering over a make-shift helipad, dropped packets of food, items of daily necessity as per a list sent through radio, and the much awaited mail from home – it was a red-letter day for the men. It was also the 'bathing-day'. Water in jerrycans would be heated on a kerosene stove and the men would bathe protected from the biting wind by a rocky overhang. Of course, it had to be a sunny day. Having come from 'civilisation' – if our billets at Leh could be so distinguished – we declined a share of the scarce warm water and set off on a Jonga towards out next destination, *Daulat Beg Oldi* (*DBO* for short).

Soon we were at the confluence of the Rivers *Shyok* and the *Chip Chap*, the latter flowing down the *Kun Lun Ranges* in the *Aksai Chin* – the area occupied by the Chinese – and as stated earlier, traversing through the *Depsang Plains* from East to West to join the former at its origin. Since truth must prevail, it must be stated here that in the summers – if the maximum temperatures of minus 5 to 10 degrees Centigrade that prevails in this region could termed as 'summer' – the 'rivers' and the 'confluence' are but ankle deep trickles of water flowing leisurely along a couple of streams just a few feet wide. Come the month of October and the entire landscape would be blanketed with snow cover and remain so till early Jun or so. I stooped down to take a sip of the cold and hard water – "A confluence of rivers is a gift of God", the 'spirits' had suggested to me.

Sketch 2: Karakoram Pass is Marked by a Brown Stone Tablet Embedded
on a Stone Cairn

Following the bed of *River Chip Chap*, we reached the camp at *Daulat Beg Oldi* in the early afternoon. Situated on an open plateau 5100 meters (16,750 feet) high and straddling another confluence of a barely distinguishable stream that runs down from the *Karakoram Pass* and the *River Chip Chap, Daulat Beg Oldi* is an exotic location. But more about it later. Presently, with the better part of the day at our hand, I decided to fulfill my childhood dream of standing at the fabled *Karakoram Pass*. We turned North and followed the stream up the gradient, stopping well short of the Pass and covering the final stretch on foot.[7] (See **Sketch 2**).

Karakoram Pass, 5400 meters (17,700 feet)

It was an exhilarating sight, as standing next to the stone cairn which marks the Indo-Tibet Border, I gazed Northwards along the valley and over the skyline to make out the course of Rivers *Yarkand* and *Wahab Jilga* and the 5000 meter (16,400 feet) high table–top like plains of *Chumit Tang*[8] in Tibet that sprawls yonder. I tried to visualize as to how it must have been in the centuries gone by, when '*Malik Shah*' was a prominent halting place for the trading caravans. With '*Khimas*' (tents) pitched up or rented from the '*Sarai Maliks*' (inn keepers), the tired beasts of burden – the double-hump camels and Ladakhi ponies – unsaddled and let off to feed and water, '*Langars*' (eateries) churning out delicacies to starved palates, a makeshift bazaar of exotic and mundane goods, music and dance under the skylight; it must have been a '*mela*' (fete'). By tradition, such halts were known by the name of the Sarai Malik or the man who ran the Langar. But what was Malik Shah or Abdul Gafoor, or the one known simply as the '*Hazi*' like? How did they live? When did they flourish? .... You might find an answer if you speak to some of those ageless old men of faraway *Turtok* or *Skardu*. Duly chastened thus of my insignificance in the scheme of the eternal nature, we returned to *Daulat Beg Oldi* to halt for the night.

Daulat Beg Oldi is named after a prominent caravan-merchant's wife, who undertook to accompany her husband in his travails. It is here somewhere hidden within the closet of time that this remarkable lady had breathed her last. She lies buried among a cluster of nearly obliterated graves spaced on a high ground above the camp. The Army camp consisted of a few prefabricated shelters and some ruins of stone masonry which might have been a part of the Army post in 1962, or might even have served as a *Sarai* or a *Langar* during the days of the caravan.[9] After a frugal meal and some usual army talk with the post commander, we went off to sleep.

Double Hump Camels Ruminating, in Nubra Valley

It was a full moon night. I woke up with start. I was sweating inside my sleeping bag and my heart was thumping so loud that I could actually hear it. As always, I had avoided going through the boredom of acclimatization, dismissing the risk it entails at such extreme high altitudes. "Luck seem to have run out this time", I mused. An urge to empty the bowel was another sign that reinforced my apprehension that my time might be over. Out of the makeshift toilet, I went out in the open, sat down leaning against a rock and waited for the matter to go worse; there was no way out of such situations.

The dust-free air and the snow capped surroundings had rendered the moonlight as bright as a subdued Sunny day in the plains. I could see

Tea Break at Karakoram Pass

30, 40 or 50 miles around me, bathed in milky white and enveloped with silence so complete that made one lose himself. As the reader might have guessed of course, nothing came of this episode, and soon enough I engaged myself in communicating with the 'spirits' of the martyred Jat Regiment soldiers who were said to be still holding their post to thwart any further intrusion by the Chinese, and were reputed to be rather rough with any delinquent sentry in the camp. Indeed, they seemed to have succeeded; the Chinese did not venture close. I saluted these sentinels and went back into the shelter and into my sleeping bag.

DAY 4: DEPSANG LA – BURTSA GONGMA

Daulat Beg Oldi, 5100 meters (16,750 feet)

Our Northward journey along Route 1 having been completed, we now headed Southwards on our return journey along Route 2 across the vast *Depsang Plains*. The 5300 meters (17,300 feet) high plain-land is flat all around, with some well rounded and gentle hillocks here or there. The surface is made of hard, compacted gravel and so one can drive unrestrained at 80 kilometres per hour in any direction ! We drove past some relics of the 1962 War which still lay scattered all around – some bunkers, frame of a crash landed helicopter and empty as well as 'live' cartridges and ammunition shells. Individual soldiers' accoutrements – a boot here, a belt there, an ammunition pouch elsewhere – lay scattered marking the spots where the army men, having expended their meagre issue of ammunition, had sallied out of their trenches to engage the attackers in mortal hand-to-hand combat till they were overwhelmed by the superior force. Another lump in my throat.

We drove over the old Dakota landing strip, the highest in the world but unused since 1962, and stopped for a quick lunch of tea, biscuits and chocolates at a post referred to as the '*Track Junction*'. The 'Line of Actual Control'[10] runs just a few kilometres to the East where goes on at frequent intervals, a ritualistic 'show of presence' between the Indian and the People's Liberation Army (PLA) troops.

I asked one of my platoon commanders, who was to proceed on leave, to join me and we took off again. After a wild, carefree drive on a Jonga over the plain-land, we arrived at *Depsang La* (5450 meters, 17,800 feet) just before noon. That was as far as a vehicle could go. Hereafter, the old caravan trail runs through a series of steep cuttings and gorges between this point and the next camp site at *Morgo*, two day's march from *Depsang La* (see Sketch 1). At this Pass, Tashi Norbu had arranged for a Ladakhi pony from ITBP to carry our rucksacks up to *Morgo*. It came from the *Daulat Beg Oldi* Camp and being an extremely hardy local 'lad', made our journey a bearable experience.

The trail took us straight into a narrow and extremely steep gorge about 200 meters deep, and we had to tip–toe over a steep and frightful descent of 30 to 40 degrees incline to reach the bottom (See **Sketch 3**). The dry river-bed valley starting at the bottom of the gorge was wide and enclosed by nearly vertical mountain wall on either side. The gradient in this vale was gentle and we moved at a good pace. Soon enough we passed another caravan camping place of the past – '*Qizil Langar*'. The location

Sketch 3: Looking book from South to North, the U-shape of Depsang La is seen on the skyline. Just below is the gorge and the steep trail to its left. Qizil Langar is near the massive rock seen in the middle ground.

of the Langar was still discernible; a massive rock with a prominent overhang preserved the signs of cooking fire. There was a strip of snow-melt water flowing next to it.

The rest of the trek was uneventful but for the revelation that some of the tennis ball like stones were in fact, once living under-sea organisms; these actually weighed like a tennis ball rather than a stone of that size. I picked one up as a souvenir, just as I had done 22 years ago at *Baralacha La*, *Kio Dhura* and *Bancha Dhura*, an equally formidable group of 17,000 to 18,000 feet high passes on the Indo-Tibet Border in *Joshimath – Darchula* Sector of what now is the State of *Uttaranchal* after its bifurcation from Uttar Pradesh. The ball-like fossil from Ladakh today shares a show case with the fossils of pieces of lizard tail and sea–shells from the Central Himalayas.[11]

Sunset found us at *Burtsa Gongma*, another camping place. There was a semi-circular 'dent' in the Western mountain wall. The protection it afforded had enticed our predecessors to construct a stone–mud random masonry hut for shelter. There were three small, dark-and-stark rooms, warm and comfortable, each with one small 'window' covered with transparent plastic for light. A stone masonry sleeping platform and a table improvised out of 'skid-boards'[12] made up for the furniture, while the roof and the doors were made up of corrugated galvanised iron sheets. One room had an attached toilet made out of used parachutes where a 'bore-hole' served as a dry receptacle. As usual, there was a jerrycane full of kerosene, a couple of lanterns and some coking pots available in the hut. A natural spring sprouted a few meters away and that completed the serene picture; it was a 'seven star' facility after an arduous march.

I wrote my notes and read a few pages till I was offered my dinner of hard-boiled rice and tinned meat, duly warmed up by Tashi Norbu and the pony-master. Then I slept; I was tired. Age was catching up – not many of my age found the need or the urge to venture on such a trip. The 'spirits' made their customary visit in my sleep and we had a long and very informative exchange of ideas; it might well have been a case of hallucinations that one has to go through in such altitudes.

DAY 5: MORGO – SULTAN CHUSHKU

Burtsa Gongma, 5100 meters (16,700 feet)

Marching twenty-plus kilometres at that altitude, most of it over loose pieces of stones, is a difficult venture. So we set off early after a breakfast of tea, biscuits, chocolate and fruit juice. The trail ran astride a nullah bed and the steep rise of mountains on either side gave a claustrophobic effect. The pony, carrying our rucksacks, was however quite 'at home' here. Unlike his clan elsewhere, he needed no guidance or motivation to move. He set his own pace and knew exactly when and where to quench his occasional thirst; he would find a pool of water frozen at the surface, break through the crust of ice with his front hoof and drink contentedly. He did appear to have lost his cool once, when he suddenly gave a start and started running helter-skelter, throwing off our rucksacks and even my photographic paraphernalia. It took some effort to entice him to come back to our fold, while I amused myself with the thought that he might have had an encounter with the 'spirits' of his past counterparts – caravan ponies or double–hump camels ! After all, we did passed by many sites where animal bones, and even parts of frozen skeletons, were laid out in some order by their grieving masters. The bones were bleached and stone-dry though it was difficult to guess their age – it could be any time between a few decades or a few centuries. We also came across some graves of humans laid out in neat rows, sheltering those who had called it a day far away from their destination or home, far from their near and dear ones. I left a fistful of almonds and walnuts for them – these people loved their dry fruit.

Later in the day we encountered two remarkable specimens of nature's geological marvel. First one was encountered mid-way through our march. It was a natural arch, more like a short tunnel, wide and high enough just to allow us to pass through. Set against a riot of different hues of brown ridgelines, it was an unforgettable sight. (See **Sketch 4**). Unforgettable too was the experience when after a while we found that the trail, barely distinguishable even at best, was now completely lost. We decided to trudge along a rather steep mountain side without losing any height, for

**Sketch 4: The Track between Burstsa Gongma and Morgo.
Notice the Natural Arch in the Middle Distance**

that would keep us above the lost trail and permit us to identify it as it might hopefully re-appear after a while; thankfully, it did so after a few kilometres.

The second marvel was even more interesting. As we negotiated a steep climb in our approach through the last bend before reaching our next halt at the *Morgo* Camp, we gazed upon a massive India Gate–like rock sitting right in the middle of the river-bed. Solidified deposits of Jade-like greenish blue eruptions from deep inside the mountain covered most of the upper half of the rock, contrasting with the latter's dark grey colour and thus projecting a spectacle most unique. (See **Sketch 5**). The rock had fissures through which poured out boiling hot water, and with it, certain chemical compounds, that led to the Jade-like deposit over the

Sketch 5: The Zade – Rock and the Hot Spring are seen in the middle distance.
The track to Morgo runs along the ridge on the right. Morgo is close to the point
where the track disappears behind the spur running from right to left. Sultan
Chushku is located at the foot of the brownish ridge in the middle distance

rock-face. The rock was popular with the troops of the Morgo Post,
providing them with the luxury of a natural hot both in that desolate,
uninhabitable wilderness.

Morgo (4500 meters, 14,750 feet) sits on a sandy valley of a subsidiary
nullah running down the glaciers to its North and joining the main course
of the *River Shyok* some distance South of its location, at a place known
as *Sultan Chushku*. A look at Sketch 1 would also highlight the importance
of *Morgo* astride the old caravan route. Besides the Routes 1 and 2, there

The Trail to Morgo

was also a third route to Xingjian. Rather than turning Northwards at *Diskit* into the *Nubra Valley*, this route followed the *Shyok Valley* throughout, skirting the *Karakoram Ranges* and passing through the ancient villages of Agham, Darbuk and Shyok, before joining up with Route 2 at *Sultan Chushku*. This Route, though longer, did not involve crossing of the formidable *Saser La*. *Morgo* was also well ensconced and protected from the elements and had a sprawling camping ground – there also was, of course, the lure of the hot springs of the Jade-Rock nearby.

Presently, *Morgo* was a permanent camp of the ITBP and a small detachment of Army. The ITBP camp was a remarkable feat of ingenuity. There was a massive dump of empty jerrycans, parachutes and skid-boards, items used for air-dropping of supplies, which had accumulated over the decades, there being no means of returning these for re-use. Troops, therefore had made the best use of these materials. Huts were made of jerrycan walls and floors, skid– boards provided for doors, ventilators, benches and tables, and used parachutes, besides catering for canopy-type roofs, lined the walls and floors to provide a finish which could compete with any well appointed room elsewhere. The air-gap within the jerrycans and the insulation from the parachute material kept the huts warm and cozy.

We were hosted by the ITBP Company Commander – a veteran officer who has seen much service under similar conditions – and partook of a delicious dinner in his hut while a battered transistor radio belted out popular Hindi songs. Then we returned to our huts and slept.

DAY 6: THOISE

Morgo, 4500 meters (14,750 feet)

This day we were to turn Westwards to halt at *Saser Brangsa*, the point where Routes 1 and 2 bifurcate and from where we had taken Route 1 to start our Northward journey six days back. The sand and stone riverbed from *Morgo* to *Saser Brangsa* was pliable by vehicles. A para-dropped '1 Ton'[13] vehicle – so ramshackle that it was difficult to believe that it was not a junk – was placed at our disposal and we took off after a hearty breakfast, courtesy the good men of the ITBP. Two hours of bumpy, bone-shaking ride later, just as we were approaching *Saser Brangsa*, came the message over radio that a medium helicopter of the Air Force was being flown-in to *Morgo* to deliver some supplies and to get us back to the local formation headquarters near *Thoise*. We retraced back to *Morgo*.

Tashi Norbu had decided to stay back to complete his tenure and I bade him good-bye, volunteering to sent him some of his photographs. Soon enough, the helicopter came and made a drop run along the sandy riverbed. Then as it hovered a few feet above the ground, I pulled myself into its open hatch. I waved at the expressionless pony and his equally nonchalant master, and we took off.

At 1200 PM on Day 6, we arrived at the headquarters. A few weeks later, I posted some photographs to Tashi Norbu. There was no confirmation of its receipt.

Postscript

Ladakh today is a hot tourist destination. The process of confidence building measures with China has eased the tension, baring occasional flare ups and construction of a motorable route astride the *Shyok Valley* upto *Depsang La* has commenced. Meanwhile, the air-strip at *Daulat Beg Oldi* has been rehabilitated.

May be in my life–time, I can go there one again. Wishful thinking and distant dreams keeps us going, don't they?

NOTES

1. 'La' means a pass.
2. The trade interaction between these diverse regions had led to the gradual spread of Islam among the Buddhists. This is evident from the Buddhist traditions in vogue among the Muslims even today.
3. A Jeep–like vehicle, extremely powerful and versatile, that served the Indian Army during 1970's till the early 2000's.
4. The convention was that you were expected to leave as much of the fresh stuff that you might have consumed, for those who follow.
5. That reinforces, in one way, India's claim over Aksai Chin based on the principle of Watershed. If the River rises in Aksai Chin and flows down towards the West into undisputed Indian territory, it is obvious that the Watershed lies in that region. But then the Chinese logic has been always so exasperating.
6. This was notwithstanding the fact that running these vehicles in such altitudes and temperatures was not easy; one had to put up with the problems of starting and lubrication with frozen fuel and lubricant, loss of engine power, lack of spares and reduced service life.
7   One imagines that traditionally, our Mother India wears a beautiful crown. The Karakoram Pass and the Indira Col to its West are located on that crown. Obviously, I was very happy to have been there. Years later I also got an opportunity, thanks to the ways of the Army, to touch the Indira Point, the South-most tip of India that forms a part of the Andaman and Nicobar Islands. Seen in light of the rest of my service, I have virtually crawled all over our Mother India.
8   'Tang' means plains.
9. *The crisp, sanitized high altitude air being devoid of living organisms – including the humans – structures and objects remain undisturbed for centuries in this region, and therefore, it was hard to guess the correct vintage.*
10 A rough 'Line' separating the areas under the control of the Indians vis-a-vis the Chinese, without prejudice to the settlement of the final alignment of the boundary, when it comes.
11. Eons ago, a sea separated the Indian landmass from Tibet. As the former closed

up due to tectonic movement Northwards, push caused the sea bed to rise, thus forming the Himalayas. The geography reinforces this theory. The salt-water lakes – including the massive Pangong Tso and the Tso Morari – are but remnants of the sea-water that was trapped within the natural bowls of the hill-sides. Most of the seawater however, had found ways to drain down-slope towards the South. The massive outflow over the following thousands of years led to creation of the wide riverbeds and deep gorges. Today these have little more than trickles of snow-melt water flowing through.. Evidence of smaller lakes in various stages of draining out – a lake shrinking, a marshy bed, a moist depression – are seen as one moves Northwards. The thought of a trekker thousand years hence finding mash-land in place of a lake and dry depressions in place what is a mash-land today, was amusing ! Fossils of the sea–life found in this high-altitude desert is another heritage of this region's past.

12.   Ply board, designed to form a platform over which supplies are secured with straps for safe para–dropping.

13.   A small, versatile truck of one ton capacity, in service with the Army till it was discarded in early 2000, and which routinely carried incredible loads of men and material.

*

6

Star TV: Rifleman Santa Singh's Diary

Motor Sport is a very good sport. In olden days it used to be known simply as motor racing but now a days its scope has enlarged many folds and hence the current nomenclature. 'Formula Racing' is one of the interesting aspects of Motor Sports. This is a very peculiar ritual in which weird looking vehicles run around in circles, apparently chasing some bad character who is trying to run away with an important 'formula' which could devastate the world. But more about this later.

Coming back to 'Motor Sport'. As I said, it is a very good sport. It involves three men and a large crowd. The men wear colourful dungarees that are completely covered with logos of the world's entire automobile industry, so much so that it is difficult to judge the actual colour of the overalls. So dressed, these three climb up a podium and pick up 5 litre bottles of a white liquid. Now the actual game begins. The three drench themselves, each other and even that part of the crowd which is within range, with spray of this white liquid amidst loud noise, clapping and frantic leaps. Every one – the participants as well as the crowd – howl, shout, grimace and jig about but it is very difficult to know if it is in protest or in joy. Sometimes the number of participants on the podium is reduced to two only when one of them gets hurt in the process of giving what is known amongst the professionals as the 'accident shots'. What follows I do not know, because at this point the TV changes the topic and enlightens us about some Hotel in Hong Kong where good liquor is served near – guess where – a swimming pool ! It must be an 'in' thing to use swimming pools for drinking sessions rather than for swimming; things have changed since I left the civil surroundings.

Motor sport has an interesting prelude. Just prior to the liquid spraying spree, the ritual of 'Formula Racing' is gone through. Whether the bad character running away with the 'formula' is caught or not, is difficult to know. What is known, is that the chase comes to an end when a hefty character leans over the fence and frantically waves a black and white chequered flag. At this signal, the participants of the chase are supposed to halt, pump their fists in the air, do a jig and even start crying – probably because the bad character had got away. The actual sport them follows – spraying of white liquid.

Another interesting part of the ritual are the 'accident shots'. Some participants collide with each other to provide the TV crew with opportunities to take these shots. At great speed, these shots are most amusing; in fact the audience eagerly awaits these visuals more than anything else. Accident shots are the earners of revenue and the main source of funds for the white liquid – the entire event in fact.

As India 'opens up', politically, economically and literally, one hopes Motor Sport too would come upon us soon. While we would see it 'live' and thus learn as to what exactly happens after the liquid spraying, *satta* dons, I am told, will have a field day raking in profits. To quote our Finance Minister who visited us recently, there will be improvements all around.

Amen!

Postscript

Formula 1 Racing has indeed come to India. It is however, not known if Santa Singh could witness the spectacle of the race that took place at Greater Noida in 2012. Nonetheless, almost all those who call themselves, and are called by their jesters, as 'celebrities' had made a bee-line for the event. No, the purpose was not to understand or enjoy the sport; it was to get photographed doing silly things near the race track.

*

7

The Shoe Rack

It was the first ever piece of furniture he had bought. It had since then occupied a special place in his heart, so what if it was cheap and ugly.

In his middle class family, a boy had one pair of shoes, with laces, black in colour. Slip-on shoes without laces – known as the 'pump shoe' – were generally associated with debauchery and *Zamindari* (landed aristocrate who as a class were generally considered to be of easy virtue, not without reason) while one was considered a rebel of sorts for opting to buy brown coloured shoes. Rarely, if ever, such a chance came one's way in any case, for buying shoes was a big occasion, coming once in two or three years and rightfully presided over by the family elders. It was too serious an investment to be left to the 'young' – a term which meant yet unmarried.

One also had a pair of *chappals*. Shoes were for strictly formal occasions, such as wedding or school admission, while the chappals served the semi-formal ones, such as visit to relatives or bazaar. Rest of the life was spent blissfully in the barefoot. If, therefore, those seven pairs of different types of footwear that were thrust upon him as he entered the military academy had caused him considerable amusement, that should be understandable. Some time later, owning a shoe rack on which would gleam rows of boots and shoes, became a very desirable prospect for him.

It was during the Young Officers course that he found the opportunity to acquire one. A small rack of three tiers, made of discarded timber scantling and costing a stiff Rs 7/- plus 75 paise for its transportation, was finally installed at his bachelor's den one late evening. With much excitement, the array of boots and shoes were assigned to their hierarchical positions, the top left going to the thirteen nail 'ammo' boot 'number one' that was meant to be worn, with utmost deference, for the 'drill parades'. Of course, the lowly chappal had to settle for the bottom right hand corner, at the very end of the order. One day arrived the 'Half-Wellingtons' – beautifully crafted ankle boots with a 'box' fitted into the heel to fix equally well crafted riding spurs – a part of the 'blue patrol' dress. Obviously, it displaced the drill boot to the second place.

That was till he was married.

In his turn, a house was allotted to him. Few days later, he was horrified; dainty, colourful and in fancy designs, as many as three pairs of feminine shoes rested upon the top tier of the shoe rack ! The drill boots had been consigned to the floor, as were few others, while the chappals had been banished altogether – these were later located under the bed. Horror of horrors ! Sanctity of the hierarchy of boots had been tampered with. Good God !!

Few years down the line, steadily, the shoe rack started slipping away from his possession. As time passed by, most of it was filled up with shoes of growing up kids, a boy and a girl, with just the last slot – originally occupied by the master's chappals – still remaining reserved for the lady of the house. His military as well as civil footwear managed to be parked in some corner, some nook. They survived somehow, yet shining, and worn with unflinching pride, as before, even if stoically braving the neglect and indignity from the rest, 'civilians' as they were. Regretfully, the favourite shoe rack had, by then, gone completely out of his hand.

Many years passed. Of the old lot, only the Half-Wellingtons survived, while others were turned over. The 'ammo' boot was replaced by the effeminate 'DMS'. Weathering the ups and downs of a soldiers life, he was, what was generally referred to as, 'doing fine'. And as the home run to retirement began, the son – a strapping six footer now – left on his own devise of life, to chart his own course. For many days the shoe rack remained half empty. Then, gradually, shoes of the lady retrieved their lost positions and returned to find a place on the shoe rack, alongside the daughter's footwear.

More years passed and then it was time for the young lady – bright and beautiful – to start her own life.

Twenty five years after they had lost it, the man's boots got their rightful places back. Somehow, he could not rejoice at this gain. Indeed, it seemed to him that he had lost something. The silly fellow.

*

8

The Battle for Jaffna

The Beginning

The proverbial Indian Army characters, *Sepoy Bhup Singh* and his '*Kaptan Saab*' felt somewhat uneasy. Neither had seen or heard anything like this before. The benign allies of yesterday had suddenly turned into a ruthless adversary. There were no battle lines, no positions, no attack or defence, no air or artillery bombardment. Worse, there was no defined enemy. The soldiers didn't like it at all.

In the beginning of October 1987, the Liberation Tigers of Tamil Elam (LTTE), the most dominant Tamil military group, had dropped its pretensions of accepting the Indo-Sri Lanka Accord that was sealed between the two prime ministers, Rajiv Gandhi and Jayawardane, to bring peace among the warring groups, the ethnic Sri Lankans and the Tamils, under the supervision of Indian Army. Mass suicide of its leaders arrested by Sri Lanka Army, to avoid transportation to Colombo for trials, provided the spark. The LTTE had then re-imposed the state of war, and had let it be known that any action by the Indians to challenge their control over the Tamil majority areas would invite unrestrained retaliation.

Jaffna is the nerve centre of Tamil affairs. Barring the small seventeenth century Dutch Fort which sheltered a beleaguered unit of Sri Lanka Army, and recently joined by a peace keeping detachment of the Indian Army, the entire Jaffna Peninsula was under control of the LTTE. This control had to be wrested back if the *Indian Peace Keeping Force* (IPKF) hoped to dictate the issue of peace in terms of the Rajiv-Jayawardane Accord. Additional troops were therefore inducted into the Peninsula through the *Palaly Air Base* and the *Kankesanthurai Port* from where they were ordered to advance towards Jaffna Town, 20 kilometres away. Time was of essence, and therefore, units were mustered hastily, landed at Palaly and Kankesanthurai, and ordered to move post- haste, without any worthwhile preparation. Neither the LTTE, nor its ominous military threat was taken seriously.

The Shock

With the IPKF detachment and the Sri Lanka Army garrison bottled up inside the Jaffna Fort, ringed on all sides by the LTTE and subjected to their continuous fire, the situation was fast becoming critical. Control of Jaffna therefore became the main objective of political and tactical importance. The operations were to be conducted under the overall control of HQ 54 Infantry Division located at Palaly, with lightly armed battalion size elements which were mustered hastily from 41, 91 and 115 Infantry Brigades, 41 and 115 Infantry Brigades having been re-orbatted from 4 and 36 Infantry Divisions respectively. Thus the operations began with units coming from different formations without any time given to integrate themselves into a composite field force. The sense of urgency was interpreted as a license to disregard the fundamentals of reconnaissance, deliberate planning, balanced composition and grouping of forces and adoption of correct tactics; an atmosphere of dealing with a weak enemy in 'jiffy' prevailed.

On 7-8 October, a pre-emptive but poorly planned attempt to neutralise the LTTE Headquarters in Jaffna by landing a company of troops by helicopters on the open grounds of Jaffna University failed with considerable losses. Departmental buildings located all around were

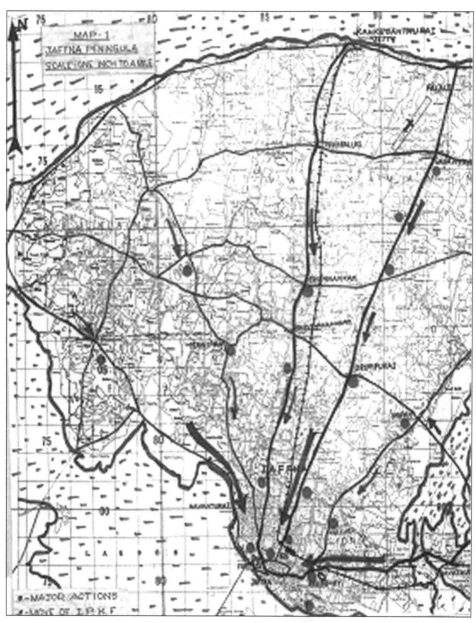

Advance from Palali – Kankesanthurai to Jaffna

held by the LTTE who directed a rain of fire upon the exposed troops, decimating the company despite a valiant fight put up by them. Consequently, by mid October, three columns – one from each Brigade – were hurriedly assembled and ordered to move astride the roads running into Jaffna from North-West, North and East with the aim of liberating the town. Almost immediately, all three ran into fierce opposition.

Jaffna is a sprawling township consisting of an unending carpet of single storey houses packed close together. Sandwiched between the rows of houses run the roads towards the town centre. The situation was ideal for use of sniping and mining to oppose a military advance. The LTTE used these two methods to devastating effect. The IPKF, as stated, was ill prepared for any deliberate military action – naively taking their 'peace keeping' role rather literally. Thus departing from all tactical norms, they had dispensed with grouping of their medium or heavy weapons and relied only on their light weaponry to deal with the supposedly *'riff-raff'* Tamil army. In another amateurish violation of the fundamentals, armoured vehicles were pressed into the advance over the constricted space of narrow roads with the hope of impressing the rebels. In the event, these hulks of manoeuvre warfare became sitting ducks for the well sited Improvised Explosive Devices (IEDs) laid by the LTTE and covered with direct fire from the safety of flanking buildings.

As the columns advanced hurriedly along the narrow roads lined with houses, they were frequently subjected to sniping and automatic fire by the LTTE cadres who would vanish at the first signs of danger to themselves. Once in a while, an IED would be detonated under a worthwhile target, generally the armoured and troop carrying vehicles, by a firer hidden a safe distance away. The melee, which ensued among the ill-prepared troops hemmed in by the closely packed built-up area, would then be subjected to intense automatic fire, followed by a vanishing trick – in all a highly demoralising and frustrating experience for men used to more conventional forms of combat. Thus, a series of such actions in close succession slowed down IPKF's advance towards Jaffna to a crawl. As the casualties rose, recourse to basic tactics was gradually – albeit

Map 2 : Capture of Jaffna Fort and Town

reluctantly – adopted and with abundance of courage, the advance continued.

The Link Up

Three battalion size columns advanced along each of the three converging axes (see Maps 1 & 2). Throughout the move, there was no let up from constant harassment by the cunning enemy which resulted in the battalions undertaking a series of small but intense and violent 'clearing' actions along the routes. On 19 October, the North Western Column, moving along the coastal axes, fought its way to the beleaguered Jaffna Fort. The Eastern Column then captured the historic 'Residency' complex which was being used by the LTTE as their training centre. This was followed by clearance of the Jaffna Railway Station. By 23 October, the

Northern Column had also reached the Fort after dealing with constant opposition on the way, thus affecting a link up with the other two columns at the battle-devastated town of Jaffna.

Consolidation

Though Jaffna had been captured, the situation was far from being under control. As the advancing columns moved ahead, the vacated positions along the routes were re-occupied by the LTTE. The situation was such that effective control of IPKF in Jaffna Peninsula was limited just to the areas around the Palaly Air Base, the Kankesanthurai Jetty and the Southern parts of Jaffna Town.

Beginning from the last days of October 1987 till the end of the year, the IPKF, in a series of deliberate small scale operations, slowly and the gradually assumed a near-total degree of control over the Jaffna Peninsula. Complete control of all areas was, however, impossible in an insurgency environment, more so in the face of a highly committed adversary such as the LTTE. Jaffna, due to its political importance, however remained in a perpetual state of war till the end of 1987. The thickly built up area provided to the LTTE ideal opportunities for sniping, lobbing grenades into IPKF vehicles and positions, booby trapping of IPKF routes and positions, and engage in 'fire-and-run' actions. No day or night passed without an incident. There were even attempts to crash explosive loaded vehicles into IPKF positions. Handling such situations was tricky and required utmost patience, cool courage and deliberate, well thought out, plans of action. It goes to the credit of the IPKF that they assumed their professional composure and established their control over such a difficult situation in most professional manner. Even more remarkable was the conduct of IPKF personnel. During the daily routine of 'cordon-and-search' operations, security checks at main roads, and against constant provocations from LTTE cadres, the IPKF personnel kept their cool and always acted with restraint. Had the Sri Lanka Army displayed such traits in the first place, probably the ugly civil war would have been averted.

The end of 1987 saw the IPKF in effective of control over the Jaffna

Peninsula. Realisation that IPKF meant no harm to those without weapons, brought the population trickling back into the town. Commercial activities started and life returned to near-normal. Battered and bruised, the LTTE took refuge into the jungles of *Vavuniya* to the South of the Peninsula to bide their time.

The Army's Civic Role

'Operation Pawan', as the IPKF's deployment in Sri Lanka was codenamed, was remarkable on two counts: one, it brought the vicious civil war under control to foster peace in the people's routine life; and two, it reconstructed and rehabilitated the civil society to make it stand up again. Indeed, remarkable in its efficiency was the manner in which the infantry troops and their support elements brought about a swift end to the ruthless rule of the LTTE in North and North-East Sri Lanka, notwithstanding the casualties that it suffered at the beginning. On the civic action front, even providing for their traditional motto of '*Sarvatra*' (being omnipresent in action), the role played by the *Sappers* in Sri Lanka had been larger than life. This was due to a combination of a water-obstacle predominant terrain and the enemy's tactics of fighting through explosives, which required the 'Engineers' to be at the fore-front of all military actions. Even the IPKF Reserve engineer regiment, which was inducted for 're-construction and rehabilitation' work in Jaffna Peninsula, had been active also in undertaking all kinds of combat tasks in close support of 'cordon-and-search', patrolling and raid operations. Besides, the responsibility of defending the most sought after enemy target – the 'Residency' and the 'Town Hall – Municipal Library Complex' – which became the seat of the local government functions in defiance of the LTTE's diktat – had been given to a company of this regiment. During the following two years, under an elaborate re-construction and rehabilitation scheme, the *Sappers* made functional the hospitals, roads and railways, electricity and water supply, schools etc., while other units of the IPKF undertook to restart bus services, banks, schools, and distribution of rations and medicines.

The IPKF was highly successful in ending the unrestrained cycle of violence perpetrated by the LTTE as well as the Sri Lanka Army and restoring normal life. Thus a war-like situation was brought under control to the extent it was feasible in an indigenously born insurgency situation, much to the relief of the common man. That made people – the LTTE included – respect the IPKF.

Towards Normalcy

At the end of October 1987, Jaffna was a ghost town of demolished buildings and defunct civic amenities. Restoring normalcy in this war ravaged town was an essential aspect of peace keeping operations. Towards this end, the Herculean efforts of the IPKF started producing results, and by the middle of December, electricity, water supply, hospitals, post offices, municipal services, rail and road transport etc. were made functional. This paved way for the population to get on with their lives. By the beginning of 1988, schools and banks had opened and commercial activities had re-commenced. Soon, the situation was stable enough for the elections to be successfully conducted.

Return of the IPKF

The transition from peace keeping duties to serious confrontation with a ruthless enemy was an extremely difficult process. It was to the credit of the Indian soldier that he resolutely went through this transition with a sense of purpose as only he can. He suffered losses sagaciously, took the conflicting requirements of fierce actions and humanitarian compassion in his stride, and tackled extremely delicate situations involving rebels, politicians and refugees with remarkable resilience. His achievements were of such effect that an overwhelming majority of local population preferred to deal with him rather than having to face the prospects of return of the hated Sri Lanka Army, or even the ruthless LTTE.

By January 1988, near-normalcy had been established at Jaffna. The IPKF did well to have achieved this goal. It was a singular achievement by any standards of warfare which the misinformed polity, unable to distinguish between *military* and *political* goals, has failed to recognise. Indeed, the IPKF's success was remarkable when considered in light of the fact that it was achieved in a foreign land, and against the world's most intense civil war launched by an indigenous insurgency of fanatically committed and well organised rebel army. Total normalcy however could only come about through a political process. At this stage, with no signs of any progress on the political front and bloody incidents occurring now and then, the ethnic war had frozen to a stage of stalemate.

In 1989, *Premdasa* was elected to power in Sri Lanka. With his known aversion towards India, he asked for the IPKF to be withdrawn; in his misplaced calculation, he thought that he would then patch up with the LTTE. That mistake claimed his life – unsatisfied with a half-handshake, the LTTE assassinated him. Later, over the next two decades of see-saw conflict, the Sri Lanka Army had to struggle to recapture all those areas that were once under the IPKF's firm control, having to accept considerable losses in the process. All this while the civil society had to suffer crippling damages in terms of life, property and collapse of social order. That *political blunder*, committed just to satiate an anti-Indian urge, still hurts that country. Thus after a three year long period of military suppression of the LTTE, that yet failed to find a political resolution of the problem, the IPKF returned home in early 1990.

The state of stalemate, combined with murder and mayhem continued in this picturesque island till May 2009, when the LTTE was finally decimated. The societal cost of this twenty four year long civil war is yet to be fathomed.

The Lessons

Jumping into military operations without deliberate preparations and in disregard to the well established sequence of battle procedures that are based on historical lessons of warfare, seems to be an affliction in the Indian military establishment. Hasty committal of the IPKF in operations against the well entrenched LTTE in Sri Lanka was a manifestation of that affliction. As it can also be seen in case of the initial stages of counter-insurgency operations in the Kashmir Valley and Kagil War, whereas a few weeks of preparatory exercises would have allowed the troops to win with lesser difficulties, our urge to rush 'pronto' seems to cloud our military judgment. Moreover, we seem to have a very short institutional awareness. For example, it is usual to hear that the IPKF 'had no maps' of Sri Lanka and that initially the units had to fight with just tourist maps at their disposal, whereas actually, over a lakh maps were stocked with the military map depots! Another instance was that it was only after suffering high rate of casualties that the commanders reminded themselves of the sanctity of 'unit cohesion' and 'integrated' command and control. In similar vein, even after having borne the brunt of insurgents' sneak attacks and tactical use of the IEDs, it took yet another ten years and over a thousand casualties for us to refresh our counter-insurgency tactics and start looking for bullet proof jackets and helmets, mine protected vehicles and counter-IED equipment.

The lesson learnt is that we do not learn our lessons !

*

9

Tongue-in-Cheek: Reflections on Jaffna

It is the most beautiful place in the world – Sri Lanka. This is true in spite of its perpetually agitated people, laid back terrain and tropical climate. And Jaffna is the best place to be in, that is if one can manage to last a few days in this troubled island. Everything about this picturesque town is unique and fascinating. So much so that it has left an everlasting impression on many a soldier of the Indian Peace Keeping Force (IPKF) – literally so, in the form of war wound marks on their person – as indeed it has on the people living there in a state of penury and mental trauma.

Jaffna is a city, or is it a township or a village? No one is sure. It is surrounded on two sides by the serene yet putrefying Jaffna Lagoon. On the other two sides are situated the villages of Kondavil, Kokkuvil, Urampurai, Kopai etc, etc. It is very difficult to find out as to where exactly the town ends and the villages begin. Even the locals – hereafter referred to as the Jaffna Tamil – do not know. "How do you know where you are at a given moment ?", I once enquired of a Jaffna Tamil. "We assume to be there, where we are expected to be", he confided. Others simply pointed out, "Here, of course!". Thoroughly confounded, I kept mum.

Jaffna is covered with single storey tiled roof houses. Each house stands on a plot of land that is walled on all sides. There is invariably a gate, which opens upon a street. This allows the occupants to go out occasionally to visit friends and relatives – there being no other work – without having to resort to acrobatic feats of jumping over the walls. Since one must be loud enough to quarrel with the neighbours across the compound wall, the Jaffna women have strong vocal chords and stout necks. Every house has a garden – much to the misfortune of the men, as each afternoon, the Jaffna women complain volubly to their husbands either that there were not enough flowers in the garden, or else that there were too many of them, the man in both cases being, of course, to blame.

Each house also has a well. Besides, there are many unclaimed wells too. The Jaffna child has it in its blood not to tumble into them. In a similar situation, an Indian mother would never have a moment's peace till the children were in bed. I put it to a Jaffna Tamil once, "Did the Jaffna child by any chance ever fall into a well ?"

"Yes, he reflected, "Cases have been known",

"So what do you do about it ?", I enquired,

"We haul them out ! ",

"No, no ..., what I mean is, what do you do to prevent them falling into a well ?",

"Well, ... we pull their ears", he replied.

There are two kinds of climate in Jaffna – hot and sticky, and very hot and very sticky. The sky is clear and the Sun is harsh. Outdoor life is sheer nuisance and nerve-raking, yet it is inescapable for the men-folk who must go outdoors to take a break from being berated by their women at home. Being in such a jam from all angles, the Jaffna man is in a perpetual state of foul temper and belligerent mood. Naturally, he turns easily into a militant, up in arms against any thing and everything that he might come across. That is, till he learns to resign to his fate. It takes 30 to 35 years to reach that stage. Of course, there are many who have mastered the art of suppressing their hostile emotions. These are found staring at the infinity and smiling without any apparent cause. Some even turn to religion – though even there they are pursued by their flower-bedecked women.

Dr Rangasajahatheivasagayam – this is his short name – is a professor of history in the University of Jaffna. He is an authority on weather! Though confusing to an average human, such arrangements are quite in order in Jaffna.

"You have not had much rains this year", I suggested to him,

"Yes", he agreed,

"Aren't you worried of a drought coming up ?", I persisted, "The rainy season is almost over". "Well, its okay. It need not necessarily rain during the raining seasons", he enlightened me.

In Jaffna cars are taken out only to ferry guests, and on such occasions as wedding and funeral. Buses are boarded only for travel beyond 50 kilometres. In all other situations, the bicycle is the sole mode of transport. And it is a chivalrous society. In others words, females dominate, much to the chagrin of the men-folk, who are consigned to the fate of being the beasts of burden, with no hope of release from this bondage ever. Thus whenever there is an occasion to go from one place to another, it must be the lot of sons, husbands, brothers and fathers to keep pedalling away with an astonishing perseverance while mothers, wives, sisters and daughters perch contentedly over the cycle's front bar. The men's emaciated forms are mostly hidden by the massive proportions of their female consignments, and unless one is forewarned, he is likely to be unnerved at the spectacle. According to the "Statistical Records of Jaffna, 1988", there is one bicycle to each pair of Jaffna Tamil. Since females outnumber the males (suspected male infanticide?)by two percent, there are always some unfortunate females who have to pedal themselves. They are an object of pity in the society.

I once saw a man after he had completed transporting his would be sister-in-law to her friend's place 16 kilometres away – for gossip. I went to look at him, or rather at his remains. His head had fallen upon his chest. Every now and then he was stricken by a violent seizure when his eyeballs would turn up, teeth would clatter and body would shake uncontrollably. He was waiting for a glass of water that his would be sister-in-law had promised to bring him a couple of hours before.

From what one has learnt of the Jaffna female, it seems rather curious that their men still have the heart to consign themselves into marriage. It is, however, not only the burden of gallantry or perpetuation of their species that motivates a Jaffna man hurl himself into matrimony. He has to be enticed with suitable compensation from the bride's father – who, incidentally, also happens to be another man; either way the man is the sucker ! The compensation (they prefer to use the word "dowry") is quite stiff; rightly so. The cost of luring a doctor or a lecturer to his doom is anything up to eight lakh rupees, while that of a bicycle mechanic is one lakh. That's the rate. After the wedding, the couple is encouraged to set up home at a distant place. Thus the relatives on either side wash their hands off to their immense relief.

Employment is easy to come by in Jaffna. This has robbed the titillation and charm of looking for a job. This situation has also struck a death-knell over the age-old attraction of taking up to begging. Notably, the employed do not distinguish between personal and office work, and are devoted to either in equal measure.

"You didn't open your bank since Monday ", I enquired of the bank manager.

"Yes", he agreed, "I went to attend my neighbours niece's friends wedding". This was a good enough reason to keep the bank shut!

I once did detect a beggar at Eluthumadduval. Crowds from distant places were coming to look at him. Some decided that the character was doing it for a bet while others found various philosophical explanations to this extra-ordinary behaviour. They fed him, clothed him and allotted him some 'work'. Since the beggar made it clear that he had no intent to leave his trade, it was seen to that the 'work' did not require him to move even a finger, thus preventing him from finding any excuse to protest. They even threatened to advance him some money. Later, I learnt that the fellow had left for the distant township of Galle in Southern Sri Lanka. He couldn't bear the suffocation of over indulgence. There is a limit to everything, isn't there ?

The Jaffna Tamil is politically very active. All are committed militants and want to get a better deal for themselves. This in simpler words means that they wish to subject the majority Sinhala or the minority Tamils – depending upon the ethnic group one belonged – to organised exploitation and suppression. But alas, that is not possible due to the intolerable posture of intransigence adopted by the either of the target groups. Presently, the uncooperative Sinhala attitude has forced the Jaffna Tamil to form several militant groups on the lines of English county clubs. Name of each group is framed around four blood-stirring words in varying sequence. These words are "Liberation", "Tamil", "Eelam", and "Tiger". The exclusivity among the groups, if any, ends here. The enemies of each of these Tamil militant groups, in order of severity are : the Janata Vimukti Perumana (JVP for short, a Sinhala militant group), the government, the innocent Sinhala, members of the competing Tamil groups, and lastly, the innocent Tamil common citizen. All killings are carried out strictly in that order of precedence. Since this sort of situation is only a few decades old, the warring groups are not yet clear on their charter of demands. At times, when the whole business of militancy is threatened by government action, all the groups become pals and jointly ward off the danger. There is much camaraderie and bonhomie then – till they fall out and start killing each other again.

In 1987, the situation was further complicated by the appearance of the Indian Peace Keeping Force (IPKF) on the scene. It was a force which was compassionate towards the Tamils and yet friendly to the Sinhala. It was pro-Premdasa, and yet close to Mrs Bandarnaike, the two top political 'poles' who would have liked to cut each others' throats. Tamils were grateful to the IPKF for bringing about normalcy, the Muslims loved it for its secular characteristics, and the Sinhalese appreciated it for preventing a break-up of the country. Yet it had to engage in bloody fights every day ! Then, after each blood-letting, the maimed and the dying militants would make a bee-line for the IPKF-run hospitals ! It was indeed a quaint spectacle.

The political scene of the times is as follows (do not read too much into the abbreviated names, they do not matter): Two Tamil militant groups, the LTTE and the EPRLF are at each others' throats. The supposedly 'pro-Sinhala' – which also implies 'anti-Tamil' – JVP is killing the Sinhalese and giving food and shelter to another Tamil group, the EROS. Yet another Tamil militant group, the ENDLF, has joined up with the Tamil militants of EPRLF and ENDLP, without severing their ties with their arch enemy, the Tamils of the TELO, while the EROS is supporting EPRLF. The JVP and the LTTE are coming closer while killing each other at the same time. JVP and EPRLF hate each other, while the Tamil businessmen hate the Tamil militants of the PLOTE who specialise in looting their merchandise, even as they have to pay 'protection tax' to the LTTE. JVP is occasionally friendly with the government which, however, is mortally afraid of it. The regular politicians of the party in power – the United National Party – are wary of their ardent supporters – the hardliner Buddhist clergy, ... And so goes on the charade; while the common Sinhalese and Tamils have to pay for this.

Simple, salubrious situation, it isn't it ? Come to Jaffna !

*

10

The Jaffna Fort

Preamble

The month of October 1987 was nearing its third bloody week. As the late afternoon Sun swathed the coastal plains dotted by coconut trees and tiled roof cottages that go to make the historical township of Jaffna, a detachment of the Indian Peace Keeping Force (IPKF) fought its way through sniper fire and rubble of war to take possession of the most famous landmarks in the peninsula – the *Jaffna Fort* and the *Residency*. A long period of low key war followed, till the Tamil rebel armies – The 'Liberation Tigers of Tamil Eelam' (LTTE) being the most prominent among them – gave up in mid 1988, and escaped to hide in jungles of *Vavuniya* and bide their time.

Inquisition of the surroundings, what started as a time-pass for a bored soldier, soon became a passion. Thus started a long spiritual association, sustained by a treasure of singed heaps of books that had been retrieved by the literally inclined Tamil citizens of Jaffna from a burning public library, and which now lay abandoned in the war zone.

This then is the story of the Jaffna Fort.

The Past

The Jaffna Fort is one of the most prominent land marks of Northern Sri Lanka. It is in fact more than that. It is a symbol of authority just as the Red Fort is at Delhi. The simile however ends here, for it is neither as majestic, nor maintained in good repairs by the post-independence government of Sri Lanka. Built by the Dutch in the Seventeenth Century, the Fort stands at the Southern end of the town on the shore of one of the world's largest – and most exotic – lagoon, presenting a pathetic sight of a majestic edifice crumbling under the ravages inflicted upon it by its own people.

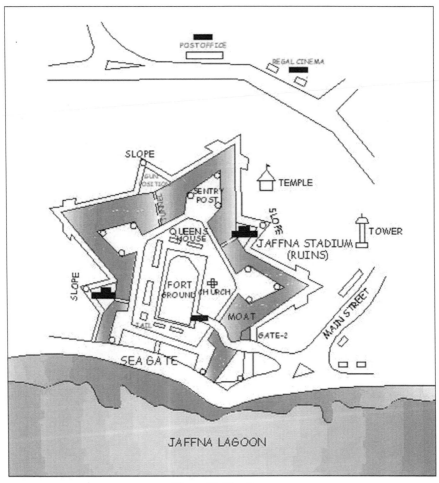

Plan of Jaffna Fort

The old Fort has had its day of glory successively under the Dutch, the British and the independent government of Sri Lanka. That was when it was the symbol of authority of the State and housed a detachment of the Sri Lanka Army under the national flag that depicts a majestic lion wielding a sword. Nemesis came in 1984, when its placid and peaceful slumber was shattered as the struggle for *Tamil Eelam* (independent Tamil homeland) graduated into an armed conflict. Seen as a symbol of the oppressive Sinhala dominated government authority, the Fort became a prized target of the Tamil Liberation *Tigers*, who laid a long and bloody siege to it. Since then it has been the last precariously held foot-hold of the government in the Jaffna Peninsula, protecting within its massive walls some irrelevant elements of the Sri Lanka Army and some police personnel from the wrath of victorious *Tigers*, who now ruled the country side. The edifice thus came to provide succour to that very establishment which had so far chosen to neglect its most basic maintenance needs. Here, the Sri Lanka Army remained completely bottled up by the Tamil *Tigers* till the 'Indian Peace Keeping Force' (IPKF) fought its way in relief on 24 October 1987. Bad days of the Fort were over, at least for the time being.

The Fort in its present from was built by the Dutch in 1680 AD; a weathered old plaque on the main entrance commemorates this event. Prior to this, during the Portuguese period (1582-1658), and even before when Jaffna was ruled by Tamil Kings, there stood a military store house at this site. It must have been a well fortified facility since it took the Dutch a siege of three and half months before the small Portuguese garrison could be induced to surrender. The Portuguese had resisted the siege valiantly but had to capitulate as food and water ran out. Their courage had so impressed the Dutch that they recruited most of these troops into their own service.

In the beginning, troops of mixed nationalities formed the Fort garrison. Following a revolt, in which the garrison commander was killed, a very harsh retribution was inflicted upon the rebellious troops by the Dutch governor of Jaffna. The mutineers were dispatched by having them

The Jaffna Fort

trampled upon by elephants, while their leaders had their hearts cut out while still alive and placed on their chest, or what remained of it. The Fort had been blooded again.

In 1802, after the Dutch withdrew from the race of colonization in South Asia, the Fort came under the possession of the British. Hereafter, with its new master in complete control of the region, it never had to face any military threat. Gradually, it transformed its character from a military outpost to that of the ceremonial seat of local administration. It remained so till the ethnic conflict between the *Sinhala* and the *Tamils* broke out in 1983-84.

Military Features of the Fort

The Fort has a pentagonal perimeter with each of its side 175 m long and made of stone masonry buttress walls 20 metres thick and 5 metres high. The rampart on top is 4 metres wide. The pentagon has its base along the sea-front while strong bastions situated at the corners dominate the surroundings. The site of the Fort conforms to the historical fact that all attacks on Jaffna had been launched from North or North-East, as indeed

An Improvised Catapult used by the Tamil Tigers to
Lob Explosive Bags into the Fort

it was even during its capture by the IPKF in Oct 1987. A 30 to 40 metres wide moat fed by sea-water protects the Fort from inland approaches on all sides. The sea – a lagoon in fact – is not deep enough for landing operations from naval crafts and yet deep enough to prevent dismounted assault. These characteristics render the Fort very difficult to attack from any direction.

There are two gates. The first, facing the lagoon, was meant for bringing in supplies, while the other, on the South-Eastern wall, was used for access in and out. The latter is actually a double gate with the moat in between. The outer gate too had a moat protecting it, probably a drawbridge too, though these have long vanished. Approach to this gate is through a narrow winding path enclosed by high walls on either side – a classical design to prevent forcing of the gate by 'ramming' that was in the practice those days. Retaining walls of heavy stone blocks strengthens the outer bank of the moat to prevent its collapse which could compromise its defence potential. It is just as well that this was done, else the moat may not have survived the years of neglect that it has been subjected to in the later years. From the outer bank of the moat, the ground slopes down on all sides for about fifty meters before it merges with the surrounding plains. This seemingly inconsequential design feature serves two very important purposes; it prevents even undetected reconnaissance of the battlements, and it renders the troops attempting to storm the Fort from any of the land-ward approaches virtually naked to the defenders fire from the ramparts.

An interesting feature of the Fort is the citing of three triangular 'screening' batteries across the moat. These were gun positions from where a mass of attacking forces closing towards the moat could be mowed down. There were tunnels passing under the moat which connected these batteries; these are now dilapidated and snake-infested. Small cylindrical pill-boxes made of stone masonry are sited at each of the turning points on the ramparts and the bastions to serve as a sentry posts. These are still in use.

In all, the ramparts, bastions, moat, and the pill boxes render the Fort much more formidable than what is apparent at the first glance. Yet, in 1802, the overall strategic situation had became so unfavourable to them that the Dutch gave it up to the British without even a whimper.

The greatest drawback of the Fort is its lack of a source of potable water. In fact, the reason for the Portuguese capitulation to the Dutch after the long siege was that the water stored in masonry tanks had finished. Indeed, there are a few shallow wells inside but the water is meagre and brackish. In modern times, the Fort had piped supply of treated water from the 'Jaffna Municipal Council Water Works'. Besides, it also had electricity supply from the power house at *Marthanamadam*. Since the out-break of hostilities, these are disrupted off and on due to frequent disruptions caused by the rebel *Tigers*.

Outside the South-Eastern gate, flanking the approach road, are two tiny structures dedicated to the Gods. One is a decorated wall with a small niche installed in which is an image of Saint John's benevolent countenance. Opposite, on the other side of the road, is a small concrete

The Main Entrance Gate

awning that shelters a carving depicting Lord Budha in deep meditation. Together with the nearby *Kovil* (temple), this trinity is a reflection of the secular nature of the locals.

Historical Buildings Inside the Fort

There are many interesting buildings inside the Fort. These are aligned along the buttress walls, with an open ground at the centre. In the days gone by, this space was used as a play ground, parade ground, and for Sunday gatherings of splendidly attired soldiers and their radiant ladies. Today it is an unkempt helipad, and some times a tennis-ball cricket ground for the bored Sri Lankan soldiers. During the days of siege, the helipad was the sole conduit for supplies. The buttress wall itself is a hollow structure providing for a continuous row of rooms facing inwards, towards the open ground. These dark, poorly ventilated dungeon type cells housed the troops, stores, rations and the armoury. Having to bear with the sultry Jaffna climate inside these cells, and harsh sun bearing down upon white skin when outside, life must have been hard to the Europeans. But then they came here on their own, money and power offering eminently preferable compensations.

The Sri Lanka Army-Tamil Tigers confrontation has left its ugly scars on each of the once magnificent buildings inside the Fort. The cross-shaped Church, built by the Dutch in 1706, is rather painful to look at – lying in ruins and a victim of vandalism. The once beautiful tiled roof has been shattered due to shelling, allowing the elements to wither away the exquisite wood work and other adornments in the building. Man as usual, has been the greater devastator – using period furniture for fire wood and breaking down doors, windows or anything that was breakable. Yet what is left – the massive brass chandelier, partially broken wood-carved Dutch coat-of-arms, the pew and the belfry – are still a bonanza for the connoisseur. Many a faithful lie buried under the floor and the marble plaques dedicated to these persons of a bygone era have interesting inscriptions in Dutch and English, summarizing a full life into a couple of lines. The atmosphere inside is eerie !

Ruins of the once Magnificent Church, Built in 1706

The Massive Brass Chandelier
Inside the Church has Somehow
Survived Heavy Shelling

The Exquisitely Carved Belfry Inside the Shell Scarred Church

The state of the garrison commanders residence, located next to the Church and known as the 'Queen's House', is only marginally better off because it has escaped human vandalism. The residences of the Superintendent of Police and the District Judge have been subjected to much lesser damage by the shelling from the *Tigers*.

The Jail, now empty, has escaped damage all together; for once, the 'sinners' seemed to have had a better destiny ! That this wasn't so in the past is testified by a sinister four columned structure – the gallows. The rotting cross-piece and the filled up 'trap well' must have seen many a life snuffed out of existence, and are probably relieved today to be rid of their gory assignment.

A tour of the Fort is incomplete without a walk along its windswept ramparts. For it is during this walk that the combined effects of the destructiveness of man and nature is seen. The fort-walls are burdened by growing *Peepul* trees which are at work in destroying the masonry work. The muck and trash filled moat still has water, thankfully providing for

The Queen's House Situated along the Rampart

The Gallows

The Moat, a Sanctuary for the Birds and Fish

amusement to the amateur anglers. The Northern bastion is the abode of an odd combination – a bombed-out structure of what was once a Club, and standing next to it, an ancient Peepul tree that cradles a *Shivalingam* in its lap. A little further across the moat towards the Jaffna town is a 'green belt' which separates the Fort with its less distinguished surroundings. In 1984, this 'belt' assumed a sinister role to keep the Tamil *Tigers* at bay from the vicinity of the Fort. It is heavily mined and overgrows with foliage. No one goes there anymore and the man's loss has been a gain to large-size snakes.

As one treads along the beaten path over the ramparts, a panorama of unusual combinations unfolds; the serene expanse of the Jaffna Lagoon to the South and the war ravaged ruins of once a highly sophisticated international telephone exchange, the *Roopvahini* (television) studio, a super market and a cinema hall famously named as the 'Regal Cinema' arrayed all around. There is also the grand colonnaded structure – but now burnt down and roofless – of the General Post Office, the highly regarded 150 years old.

Ruins of the Once Majestic Town Hall Building

The War-torn Court complex. A Mountain of Old Records and
Books Lay Inside in various Stages of Decay.

The Jaffna Lagoon, as seen from the Ramparts. A causeway Connecting the Island of Kytes to Mainland Jaffna is Seen in Middle Ground

The Moat and the Rampart. Ruins of the Exchange, the Town Hall, The Public Library and the Durajappa Tower is seen from left to right in background. In the middle ground is one of the triangular bastions with a gun emplacement

Jaffna Public Library that was burned down by the Sinhala miscreants to spite the Tamil intelligentsia, and the high domed *Town Hall* which is in a state of imminent collapse – in all a tragic sight. Amongst the ruins, however, stands almost untouched, a small temple of *Lord Muruga* and a tall, decorated *Tower* dedicated to the memory of Mr Durajappah, the popular Mayor of Jaffna – a widely respected Tamil – who was assassinated by the misguided *Tigers* in 1975. While his beloved Jaffna bleeds, the dead Mayor is past caring.

Postscript

In 1990, Sri Lanka decided to strike a deal with the *Tamil Tigers* and sought the withdrawal of IPKF – a decision she rued later. Soon enough, the war broke out again and the Fort was surrounded by the LTTE. After a vicious fight it finally fell into Tamil hands, and had to be reclaimed later by the Sri Lanka Army at great a cost. By then, however, the old structures inside the Fort as well as those along the periphery, or whatever remained of these, had been raged to the ground to satiate the all pervasive hatred that the LTTE suffered from. A heritage has been lost for ever.

Then, after a series of see-saw battles during which control over Jaffna switched hands many times, the LTTE was finally annihilated in May 2009. Jaffna is once again the seat of Sri Lanka Government in the North. But the old, charming city has been ruined – a new Jaffna is in the making.

*

11

The Case of the Missing Solution

All characters in this tale are imaginary. Any resemblance of these characters to any one living or dead is purely coincidental – Author.

"Even Russia was better", mused Mr Bond, James Bond of 007 fame.

It was a bright morning. The sky was clear blue, and a strong breeze blew across the flats of Jaffna Peninsula in Northern Sri Lanka. Bond had just finished his morning toilet in the meticulous manner that was so very characteristic of him. He had however, contrary to the usual script of James Bond adventures, failed to be surprised by a gorgeous brunette in his bath tub. This had upset him no end. On the other hand, "An upset Bond is better than a frightened one", Generalissimo Khatpat[1] had concluded the previous evening, visualising in his mind what he had seen of the local females. He had then sacked the Major who had suggested placing a local *houri* into Mr Bond's bath tub. At the present moment, he was waiting for Mr Bond to emerge from his room before inflicting upon the hapless agent a briefing on the long festering 'Indo-Sri Lanka Issue'.

After the incident of 'Shooting the Toe', Bond had been rather careful with his pet Walther PPK Automatic Pistol. Having satisfied himself that it was not loaded, he emerged into the briefing room wearing his customary wide sensuous mouth and keen eyes. His advent pleased Generalissimo Khatpat immensely, as was evident from the manner in which the old soldier enveloped the agent. Bond extricated himself from the suffocating bear-hug with some difficulty and demanded to know the whereabouts of his breakfast.

Having worked his way through his breakfast consisting of the local delicacies – the ubiquitous 'dosai', 'chatni' and 'sambhar' – a belching Mr Bond felt free to bestow his attention upon the Generalissimo who was waiting impatiently for this opportunity, hanging to the extreme edge of his chair.

> "There was an 'Accord'. It was expected to bring a 'Solution', the Generalissimo began. "But months have passed and the Accord is yet to bring the Solution. The Accord is hardly seen these days, and it is completely ineffective, while the Solution is missing altogether. You must find this missing Solution and retrieve us from this mess", he pleaded,

> "Indeed, indeed...of course...er...hum!", replied Mr Bond to this pathetic entreaty. He then closed his eyes, presumably in meditation. Unable to withstand the suspense any further, the old soldier toppled off his chair, the resulting thud reviving the Agent. He opened his eyes and serenely enquired, "But where is the girl?",

> "Which girl are you talking about?", asked the bewildered Generalissimo,

> "There is no girl involved in this case, Mr Bond". This was Colonel Sarpanda,[2] Generalissimo Khatpat's deputy and hence the object of his intense jealously. The Colonel was promptly urged to mind his own business by his boss in a very harsh language, to which the unfortunate man readily agreed. Meanwhile, Bond had already observed, "Well, that makes it an unique case in the history of worldly troubles...the pressure is too much",

> "Quite so", interjected Khatpat..., "I must proceed to the toilet at once", finished Mr Bond.

While the Agent was attending to his pressing urge, Colonel Sarpanda was whining to his boss, "Hope we haven't made a serious mistake by commissioning James Bond to solve this problem. The 'boy emperor'[3] may not like it". In his heart, Sarpanda hoped that this came true, for his own career advancement was closely linked to the downfall of his boss. "No, no ... I have already sounded His Excellency Mr Fixit[4] and he concurs", reflected Generalissimo Khatpat doubtfully.

> "Ah, there you are, Miss Fixit is a very beautiful maiden, I knew it ! There had to be female in the plot", remarked a relived James Bond smugly returning to his chair,

> "Don't be silly. This is not that beautiful lady Fixit we are seized of. This is our government's representative at Colombo, and his appearance is far too removed from that of a comely female. Once a burglar had fainted at his sight", clarified Generalissimo Khatpat. " Now shall we get down to serious business, shall we ?, gaining in confidence, he was returning to his normal stiff self,

> "Yes, of course", growled James Bond. " Where is the Accord ?", he enquired,

> "It is in a very beautifully bound file", volunteered Colonel Sarpanda. He was again promptly shut up by his boss, who had an aversion to having his thunder stolen.

> "Whose Accord is it, any way ?", James bond continued his probe,

> "It is Indian Rajiv Gandhi's and Sri Lankan Jayawardane's", replied old Khatpat,

> "Ah ... they have been fighting, eh?,

> "No ... no ... it is that Tamil Pirabhakarn and Sri Lankan Jayawardane who have been fighting with each other",

> "Strange !", observed Bond. "Pray continue".

In great details, Generalissimo Khatpat explained the problem to Bond. He informed him that the Accord was to be followed by a Solution, but even after one and a half years, many crores of rupees spent and hundreds of lives lost, this had not happened. He then proceeded to explain to Bond that Mr J had meanwhile renounced polities, and the Indians wished Mr R would do like wise; in their opinion, that could be the greatest sacrifice made by the Nehru clan for Mother India.

"The Solution is missing", concluded Khatpat ..., "You will find it for us", he ruled with an ultimate finally,

"No, not yet, General", objected the Agent. "First tell me whose Solution would it be that's missing ?", he asked,

"It was to be the solution to the age old Tamil – Sinhala problem in Sri Lanka" enlightened Khatpat,

"And how is the Accord connected to the ...er...Solution ?",

"I don't knew, ask Fixit", advised Khatpat. "Now if you are ready...". "Not yet", insisted the Agent. "And pray what is your role in this, ... well, ... affair ?",

"I am the commander of the force which Mr R uses to beat up the Tamils of Pirabhakaran", the Generalissimo's nose, swelled by immense pride, was touching the ceiling fan, well ... almost,

"But why do you have to beat them up ? Tamils have no problems with Mr R, isn't it?",

"We soldiers do not meddle in polities", by now Khatpat had assumed a sphinx-like countenance, valour and pride dripping from it. "Fixit says it is to make them honour the Accord".

"Please start with your characteristic snoopy methods without further ado, please! We have even wired your customary Saab Turbo 900 wonder-car with a time bomb for a realistic effect on your manners", pleaded Colonel Sarpanda.

A shiver went down the spine of the veteran of many bloody espionage battles. "Enough !", cried a sweating Bond. "Mr P is fighting Mr J while Mr R and Mr J find an accord, and this is expected to find a solution. And when the goddamn solution is not found, you start beating Tamils of Mr P ! Holy Goldfinger !, you expect me to buy this nonsense ? And put my head into it ? This is insanity ! I shall have noting further to do with it. Remove the time bomb if it has not already blasted off my Saab Turbo 900, do it at once !! ", Bond had taken recourse to pacing up and down and flaying his limbs in a wide arc.

The situation was going out of hand. The Bond card was not playing up. As it is customary under such situations, the boss, Generalissimo

Khatpat, performed a vanishing act with an astonishing agility for his creaking bones, leaving the messy affair to the hapless Colonel Sarpanda, his unfortunate deputy. If it came to a pass, he would volubly deny any knowledge of hiring James Bond.

> "I wanna go home, send me home. Merc'i !, ...papa !....mama !!", having deposited himself on the floor, Mr Bond was now wailing,

> "Cool down old chap. Have patient damn it! Don't weep so pathetically, its not becoming of a Bond, James Bond of 007 fame!", Sarpanda was trying to buy time. Faces of his various junior officers flashed across his mind with the sole purpose of dumping the matter into the lap of the first available victim.

Presently Captain Kopri walked in. "Elections have been held. The Solution may be found soon", he whispered into the Colonel's hairy ears.

"Well, then, that's it...young man !" Will you please drop Mr Bond at the airport?", ordered the Colonel. He then proceeded to the Generalissimo's office to inform him of the encouraging news and claim the credit for it.

On a nippy evening, Mr Bond was found singing ballads outside the airport to earn his passage home. Earlier, he had been divested of his all-purpose watch and Walther PPK Automatic Pistol by the hotel staff to recover his dues.

For once, he had been taken for ride, Bond, James Bond of 007 fame!

NOTES

1.   Lieutenant General Kalkat was the Force Commander of the Indian Peace Keeping Force in Sri Lanka.
2.   Major General Sardeshpande was General Kalkat's deputy.
3.   As Rajiv Gandhi, the then Prime Minister, was known in bureaucratic circles.
4.   JN Dixit was the Indian High Commissioner in Sri Lanka. He shared his surname with a famous film actress.

*

12

Stay Fit!

Life would never be the same again after that morning. For, on that morning, at 7 A.M. to be precise, I, finding nothing to do and nowhere to go, watched the 'Stay Fit' programme on my wife's TV. That gave me the idea – I would become a 'physical fitness expert' ! At long last I had an opportunity to find some meaning to my so far unproductive life. I got down to business straightaway.

A quick survey of the phenomenon of 'staying fit' revealed that it was the 'in thing' these days, having taken a very prominent section of our society literally by the storm. This segment consisted of sons and daughters – mostly the latter – of the very rich and successful. There could even be their mothers in that group, though they all try to look so keen and young that it was not possible to distinguish one from the other. All wanted to stay fit. Towards this end, they were inclined to get into their imported track suits and jogging shoes after the bed tea, put on some essential make up and pick up their BMWs to go to a place of historical importance. There, in the backdrop of the ancient structures, they smilingly placed themselves at the disposal of a benign 'expert', who in his turn also smiled a lot, all the while leading his pupils through a series of very extraordinary and purportedly useful 'exercises'.

Next, I turned my attention towards the 'expert', the role I was destined to play, that would bring succour to many a rich and purposeless life. I found that there were, as usual, just three essential attributes of an 'expert'. These, in the order of importance were, first, the expert should not have an easily perceptible paunch, second, he should offer his own unique set of unusual exercises which must be completely different from any other school, and third, he should not only be capable of keeping a straight face during the ridiculous postures that he makes his pupils assume, but should also flash encouraging smiles towards the camera – the most important exercise equipment – at regular intervals.

The first condition was easily met by choosing to wear 'loose and comfortable dress' that would hide the pot belly. As for devising my own set of unique exercises was concerned, it downed upon me that actually any forms of movements and postures of the body contributed towards straining of some muscle or the other. So enlightened, rigging up an exotic set of exercises was easy. I would just start off with some combination of flailing arms, legs and torso, think of any parts of the body this contortion is likely to strain, and announce these during the exercise. Then I would pass on to any other combination which came readily to my mind; to be a trend setter one need not be fixed to any routine or convention. Keeping with the latest trends of inventing exotic definitions, I would name my method of burning body fat as the 'Wholesome Rejuvenating Programme', WRP in short. All that was left now, was to acquire that attribute of suppressing the natural urge of any trickster to laugh at his victims and substituting it with encouraging smiles. This one was difficult, but was duly mastered after insistent mental conditioning.

I was delighted ! I closed any eyes and visualised as how would a typical set of my patented WRP would run: "Stand on your feet and set them one-fifth-of-your-height apart. Bring the right knee and left elbow together. Put up your left knee to your right ear. Now try to touch your forehead with your tongue. 1,2,3...., up, clap, 1,2,3. ..... Repeat ten times. This exercise tones up your back and toe muscles, strengthens your neck and relieves boredom. Next, ..." Wonderful, I just couldn't wait!

I, the inventor of the current rage, the WRP, expect to be featured by one of those vain glossy magazines soon, and become a 'celebrity'. Then someday Zee TV will feature me in their incessant programmes. For once, that stern looking wife of mine would be stumped; her firm belief that I was a scoundrel, would be shattered once for all. What joy, what bliss !

Postscript

I am informed that by putting up new hurdles to the exercising congregations at the historical monuments with each passing day, the Archaeology department fellows are making a nuisance of themselves. For 'public consumption', they are doing so in the name of 'preservation of our heritage'. But an insider tells me that the motivation actually comes from an irritating disruption to the department employee's heritage of 'hafta' collection – a kind of innocent contribution made to the department employees by vendors who are too poor to obtain what is described in government circles as the 'licence from the competent authorities'. As a result, the neighbourhood Gymnasium, lovingly called as 'the gym' has become the latest sweat-hole. New 'gyms' are springing up everywhere on daily basis, and a new trade, known as the 'trainer', has emerged to manage these. Besides displaying meaty biceps and training their victims, these trainers also need to learn to manage the business of what is known as the "cosy-coochi-koo" among the young, and not so young, folk. I am also told that the most notable change in trend, however, is that unlike the historical monument exercises, all in the 'gym' have to wear what is described – in poor taste of course – as a 'revealing dress'. That's the latest trend I was advised.

Soon, I would have fleeced enough money from the rich 'do-nothings' to open my own 'gym' in the neighbourhood.

*

13

A Battered Steel Trunk

One of the black painted steel trunks – the ubiquitous equipment of uniformed services – was emptied of his father's police uniforms and filled up with things prescribed for a cadet joining the Indian Military Academy, Dehra Dun.

It was early Jun 1969 in an obscure, dusty and noisy township in North Bihar. At 18, he was a collegian, brusque and bold, a group leader and a class sportsman, who dreamed of joining the Army and eventually be a celebrated military leader, the only question left to be decided was whether it would be in Rommel's or McArthur's mould. Obviously, he was annoyed when he saw his mother slip into the trunk an aluminium capsule containing some dry flowers that would purportedly keep him 'safe' and a 'Dalda' tin filled with 'gujjias', a kind of sweetmeat that was his favourite – till then. "Most unlike Rommel or McArthur!", he reflected irritably. In the end he had to give-in to the mother's tearful pleas, just to indulge her.

A quarter of a century went by. Having been through a succession of hard service in areas most difficult, the trunk, now battered and peeled of paint, still retained some of its old contents. Presently, having been ordered to another difficult command assignment, he pulled out the trunk to pack.

In one corner of the trunk, covered under an old county cap of his days of university cricket captaincy, lay that aluminium capsule. Curious, he picked it up for the first time. It was actually a packing for '120' film roll which was used in photography those days. It was then that something happened that he had never experienced; he was overwhelmed with a sense of melancholy, he felt a lump in his throat. He heard his long gone mother chide him as she often did, smelt her presence, even felt the warmth of her bosom. Trembling with a sense of vacuum made by her departure, he opened the capsule. Out came remnants of a bone-dry marigold, a shrivelled 'Bel' leaf, a small piece of dry coconut and a bit of ash, all tied up in a tattering piece of while fabric. Numerous instances of his escape from death by a hair's breadth flashed through his mind, and then he saw his mother casting an invisible protective web around him. She did not speak, looked at him in a detached way, and having finished placing the web, faded away.

A hefty, tough, no-nonsense, battle hardened soldier, known variously as the 'Tiger', 'Zorawar Singh', etc., sat forlorn and motionless on the floor, clutching at his mother's gift of love. If one could dare to look close, he would have noticed tears welling into those sad eyes.

He sat there for a long, long time.

*

14

Tales and Travails of Study at the National Defence College

(National Defence College is the most prestigious institute for higher learning that is reserved for the best among the top level Armed Forces and Civil Services officers. Nominated officers undergo an one-year Course when they interact with the top-most mandarins from every conceivable field)

A Misfit's Trauma

I felt sheepish. It was for the second time in my life that I wanted to hide someplace. The first time it was when they had empanelled me for promotion to one-star rank much against the run of play. Conscious of one's rather modest abilities and having done all that one could to avoid being pushed up the ladder, my peers had concluded that there wasn't any threat of further promotion coming my way – ever. That prediction didn't come true, much to chagrin of theirs, and mine. Then just as we had somewhat reconciled, came this bombshell! It was utterly humiliating to be nominated to attend this course at the National Defence College, NDC for short – reserved for the very best among the true blue blood in the Armed Forces and the Civil Services – in this manner; there is a limit to undeserved solicitations and misplaced felicitations one can bear with after all. How was I to show my face to those who knew me? The first time I had, indeed, stoically stood through the promotion bit, but this time the macabre joke was just too much to digest. Meanwhile, my wife, who is well aware of my worth, had, in fact, fainted on being told of this inexplicable development.

I protested at the indignity of being considered someone I was not, even if it was of a better description. Least of all was I willing to join the ranks of those who were much above my humble creed, and so become an object of banter and heart-burn among my actual station peer group. But none of my superiors would listen to my pleas to be spared of the agony of having to join company with the blue blooded lot. Some laughed at what they called as my 'impertinence', some dismissed it as 'nonsense' and some even became sombre at what they took to be my 'humility' ! The Engineer-in-Chief's emotive 'appeal' finally broke my back – how could I let a vacancy go away from the quota allotted to my 'mother' Corps, he had argued! Mother – 'Maa' – is a very sensitive issue in Indian cinema, er ... society, after all.

Somehow I managed to survive the first few days. Those days I often came across the very proper and dignified 'Course Members', all of whom have that 'NDC look' of majestic countenance and aristocratic bearing, who would disapprovingly scrutinise my disadvantaged form with a mix of disdain and curiosity – the God, you see, hadn't been generous with my deportment either. Their looks said it all, "Who might this intruder be ?... he does not belong here !... why is he treading these hallowed precincts ?...", etc. Thankfully, that stage passed by and the environment seemed to have reconciled to the anomaly of my presence in the exclusive environs of the NDC.

There are months to go by before my ordeal is finally over. Till then I have to 'act' my part amongst these exalted group of knowledgeable, experienced and intelligent Course Members, the 'chosen ones', so to say. So far, I haven't done badly in hoodwinking the class; all I have had to do is to keep my mouth firmly shut and present a low silhouette. Of benevolent disposition as they are, the Course Members seem to have taken my basic instinct of self preservation as a sign of wisdom !

I hope I am not 'found out'. At least not before December 2004, when I am due to return to the familiar and humble surroundings that I am comfortable with. Then I might have the occasion for a good laugh at the incredibility of this episode of my life: "*Chala Murari hero banney*" !

Empowerment... ?

You couldn't have missed it, so regularly the theme is displayed in advertisements, especially those which challenge you to buy an apartment or else be damned for ever. There is this man, on all his fours, on whose back is perched a child, purportedly his own. The child is all smiles, digging his heels into the man's ribs and 'riding' him as if he was a horse – or rather a 'donkey', a description which won't be far off the mark if a man indeed lets himself be treated thus. Then there is this woman; well 'made up', smiling from ear to ear and gleefully urging the child to 'ride' harder and so promote the spectacle. All this while the man has been ordained to keep his head turned towards the camera and wear a wide grin, which might indicate confusion, humiliation or subjugation, but happiness certainly not; its he who has to work his backside off to pay for the 'EMI' while the rest of the family enjoy what is described as, "lush green ..., parks ..., club ... ", etc, you see. Worse, the moron even obliges in participating in this cruel joke and does exactly what he is told to do !

That's what a 'happy family' is supposed to look like !!

There is another TV ad, which would be amusing if it wasn't for its ghastly intent. The wedding is over and the girl takes leave of her mother – who is dressed in a widow's white apparel – to 'claim' her new abode and all that goes with it including the groom, who is shown only in hazy outlines. The widow goes up to her room and positioning herself in front of a framed photograph of her late unlamented husband – and of course, at an appropriate photogenic angle for the 'shot' – delivers a 'well done, boy' speech to the deceased and departed hubby for having insured his life before kicking the bucket, and the insurance amount having come in handy ... ! The message for the hapless lot of living husbands is clear, "Insure and depart".

Lecture after lecture, at the NDC we are educated on the need for women's empowerment. One wonders as to who should need to be empowered !!

'Our' Europe

The foreign tour was great ! Having missed out on foreign assignments on as many as five occasions, this was an opportunity I looked forward to ever since I joined the NDC. We made the best use of it and saw as much of Europe as we could within those fourteen days on a very tight programme; no rest, only travel.

I was particularly happy to see the Europe in all its beauty and splendour. Indeed, I felt at home and very involved. After all, these grand cities, infrastructure and monuments – modern, massive, clean, efficient, beautiful – were made from our money and labour that was carried away by our colonisers. Without denying the Europeans the due credit for their scientific achievements and political guile, Asians and Africans can justifiably be proud of having paid for and laboured over centuries to build such great societies.

We were particularly happy to be able to look at our heritage; idol of the 'dancing Nataraja', Tipu's 'Tiger Toy', and Emperor Shahjehan's personal chair, etc. which are on display at the Victoria and Albert Museum in London. There were countless other artefacts which remain for us to see and appreciate, thanks to the artistically and historically inclined members of the British Empire. We Indians would have lost them anyway.

Good luck to our former masters, may they prosper ever. In fact, that is not such a big deal for them. Having already built everything that they needed – houses, offices, civic infrastructure, roads, railways, social facilities et al – from their colonial 'earnings', and which are sufficient, if not surplus, for the kind of population they have, all they have to do is to just maintain these, which they do rather well.

Democracy... Freedom!

Having been brought up with the notion of democratic lessons learnt from Western civilisations and having admired it all along, the complete absence of democratic rights and freedom of individuals in these countries came as a shock – horror in fact. In Europe, you are not free to eat where you like, walk where you want to, sleep where you wish to, throw rubbish wherever, exercise your vocal chord, push your way up a queue, enter a shop from the nearest entrance at hand, move against traffic – nothing at all that goes with our ideals of 'freedom'. You can not board a bus from any door you fancy, can not drive a car without valid licence and can not sit in railway waiting rooms after mid-night; the list of bondages is endless. One felt sorry for the hapless citizens of these authoritarian countries. In our country you can enter a bus through even the driver's cabin and can actually live on a railway platform for months on end. You may even start an agitation if some misguided elements dare to interfere with your way of life and ask you to travel inside a railway coach rather than on its roof. That's freedom !

Europeans are yet to taste the fruits of liberty !

Syndicate of Organised Crime

"There is negligible crime in European countries", I was told by a local acquaintance. Seen in proper perspective, however, with the taxes so high, entrance fee's to even the 'must see' monuments so stiff, rail tickets costing a fortune, a bottle of water costing between Rs 80/- to Rs 180/- depending on where you have subjected yourself to be fleeced at, and having to pay even to relieve yourself, one does not need any other organised mafia in Europe. The state itself is the unquestioned 'crime syndicate', arbitrarily and assiduously perpetuating unrestrained and unchallenged crime of loot and extortion upon its hapless people. Where is then the need or any scope for the likes of our small time extortionists or goons who engage in 'collections' to feed their families ? At least you can bargain with our criminals, even invoke some 'connections' to get past them through emotional blackmail, packaging it under caste, language, native place, religion, common acquaintances, sick mother, marriageable sister – any sob story would do. No such luck to our European brothers and sisters in the heartless system that they have to live in.

My sympathies. May God deliver them form the clutches of their state perpetuated extortion.

The Threat of Lasting Peace!

Ever since we landed up to attend this Course, we have been fed with an endless stream of incredibly frivolous chicanery, that is, of being made aware of the societies 'striving for peace', the need to 'avoid war' in order to prosper, and so on. At the beginning, prospects of such lofty ideals was very frightening. What happens to us soldiers, how are we expected to keep the fire burning in our hearths? "I told that brat not to join the Army and try for the Civil Services instead, these fellows would thrive even when there was no one left, or willing, to be served", I soulfully reflected upon my advice to my son and shuddered at his uncertain future.

The true colour of all this bunkum surfaced later, and after much introspection. In the contemporary period, the mankind has lived better than he had ever lived before. This period saw democracy and freedom spreading to all corners of the world; it also saw more wars and devastations than all previous centuries put together. Where would the British, the French or the Americans be if they did not win wars ?

No. Man can not live without war. He will invent a reason or a slight if he has to, but fight he must. We soldiers won't go hungry. My brat would not be unemployed. Amen.

*

15

The Prince of Rags

The child was wise for his age – three months to be precise. Clearly, he had learnt to be patient, suppressing his wants till his doting mother could steal a few moments to be with him, attend to him and hold him close to her warm bosom for some fleeting seconds of pure bliss. She would then put him down on his makeshift bed of coarse rags and tear herself away to join other workers who toiled to renovate the massive building which would accommodate officials of the state.

Having seen through fifty two summers of ups and downs in my eventful life of struggles, failures and even some modest success, I had found the routine of watching over the tedious and complicated construction work as quite an absorbing engagement. And so it was that I found myself in the veranda of the quarters allotted to me, and reclining on the old but comfortable easy chair, watched over the proceedings that went on ceaselessly just a stone's throw away. At the least it was better than doing nothing besides subjecting myself to my wife's incessant lectures on my fabled incompetence. Interestingly, having been accommodated in somewhat humbler but similar kind of buildings all my life in the course of work or fun, I could be quite harsh in my judgment over the intentions and calibre of those who made or maintained such structures whenever I had to put up with inconveniences small or big. I had not, at those times, known how difficult a job it could be, and so, my current vigil from the easy chair had somewhat chastised me and mellowed down my impatience with what I had earlier taken to be the "sheer callousness of the 'works' department". And it was then, that the daily chore of the 'prince', the labourer's baby born into a squalid world represented by the rags that he lay upon, had drawn my fascinated attention.

They lived under a polythene sheet just a few meters from the construction site; a non-descript man of no apparent worth, who I suspect, drank country liquor whenever he could steal away a few rupees from his meagre daily wage, his responsible and hardworking wife and their three months old son, the 'prince of rags', as I had named him after the coarse bundle of rags which served the purpose of his bed and cradle.

There he would lie peacefully over his bed of rags, which his mother made for him and placed over a small mound of piled earth astride the pathway. In the mornings he looked fresh and happy. His mother would have, of course, cleaned him, fed him, may even have put a black mark on his forehead to ward off evil eyes, before proceeding to earn her daily bread in the construction work. And so would the 'prince' look at the sky overhead, kick his small legs for joy, watch over the trees and the birds flying over him and sometimes even turn his head in his efforts to pick up the familiar, soothing rustle of his mother carrying endless loads of bricks and cement mix that would go to remake the building. As the day wore on, dust and noise would tire him out while flies would crawl all over his tiny and helpless body, much to his discomfiture. He would doze off and on to bear with thirst and hunger; he would probably be wet too. But he would be patient. He won't cry out like those fortunate babies who know that someone would come rushing to pamper them. He understood his mother's predicament and his own station in this unfair world.

And then, after a timeless wait, his mother would come back to him for that moment of heavenly bliss. He would give her a wide smile, catch hold of her earnings with his tiny hands and gurgle with pleasure when she kissed his bare stomach. Soon her 'time-out' would be up. Back to work she would go. Curiously, he did not seem to mind it at all. In fact, he would even give her a parting smile as she reluctantly picked herself up to go back to work.

Yes, that child of rags understood 'life' and its compulsions.

Evening would descend when the worthless father would come to pick him up – and his bed of rags of course – to follow his mother back to their 'hut'. Then he would be washed, fed, talked to, sung to and played with. In due course, his mother too would have had a bath, changed into her 'better' sari and get busy in cooking their meal of coarse rice and boiled potato on a make-shift fire burner, for which the father would have in the meantime collected some dry leaves and twigs. And then, a well earned rest, if only to gain strength for the morrow's back-snapping struggle.

I hope my 'prince' lives through the looming dangers of child mortality. I hope he grows up: how else shall we have our roads build, garbage removed, homes constructed or loads pulled ? Who else would queue up for hours to cast his vote and keep the democracy going, how else would the NGOs maintain their life style ? Yes, a few of his type would of course turn out to become 'anti-socials' as we call them, even if it beats me as to how can one ever imagine them growing up to be the protectors of this society ? What, after all, have they got from a system that thrives on corruption, inefficiency and exploitation ? In any case, they would mostly steal from those who have amassed ill gotten wealth; and that is alright by me.

There is hope though. Some indeed would become an *Ambedkar*, *Jagjivan Ram* or *R K Narayan*. Some would trade or learn skills that would provide for better beds for their children. Some day, some time, in distant future may be, there would be no 'prince of rags', and all these children of the street would be vaccinated, clothed, better nutritioned and sent to school – just to be the *children* as they should be.

Till those days come let my prince grow up, so that comfortable buildings could be built to accommodate the destiny makers, who may then be free from mundane worries to engage themselves in discussing poverty, illiteracy, disparity....

I hope I am not turning senile just to prove my wife's prophecy.

*

16

A Fateful Intervention

Fate, at last has smiled upon our good old FIFTY ONE Engineer Regiment: *Bhagayeshwari* has been bestowed upon us. It has been a saga of decades of hard toil mixed with sweat and blood before the blessing finally came. Gender equality has finally been restored, much to the satisfaction of the eternally tortured men folk. But as the regimental newsletter, 'The Chronicle' of October 1999, seems to suggest, there is some confusion and dismay among the 'Hanumans' of FIFTY ONE as to how to keep an young woman officer suitably 'committed' – that is what making life as difficult as practically feasible means in that regiment. That is one confusion that I, the old, crazy and diehard of FIFTY ONE, must clear.

Take the case of the utter misinformation about ours being a so called "male dominated" society. Only the morons or the brainwashed sods would believe in this lie. Indeed, females, in all their incarnations have been trampling upon us men and subjecting us to insensitive exploitation and emotional cruelty. Consider some examples that I offer to throw light on this unholy conspiracy of the women.

Mothers – and Grandmothers: Amitabh Bacchan demands to know from his brother, "*Mere paas daulat hai, bangle hai, gaari hai …; Kya hai*

tumharey paas?" ("I have wealth, bunglow, car ...; what do you have?").
To this, screen brother Shashi Kapoor, nose up in the air, eye scornful
and quivering Adam's apple, announces, "*Mere paas 'MAAA' hai* !" ("I
have mother!")- the moron prefers an old mother to such super-goodies
of life!! Unbelievable but true. A men are brought up, by their mothers of
course, to think in that self-deprecating manner.

Sisters – and Cousins: In response to just a cheap and ridiculously
flashy thread around our writ once a year, and we are expected, and
encouraged to stand tall, flex our muscles, thump our chests and empty
our pockets, ostensibly to protect our precious sister. God knows against
what. As I know of the sister class, the world needs to be protected from
them. That is how sisters make a monkey of us.

Wives – and girl friends: Lesser said the better. Take the case of my
friend Ronnie Pillay who was with me at the College of Military
Engineering, Pune, attending the degree engineering course. After the
classes were over, he would push start his rickety scooter, drive all the way
to Hadapsar, install Pamela on the pillion and take her to the Main Street.
There he would follow her dutifully while she strolled and window
shopped, feeling sorry al the while for not being able to buy her all that
she took fancy to. The she would be fed, satiated with fancy cold drinks
and then deposited back to her mother before the poor fellow could
return to his room late in the evening. All this at a salary of Rupees 630/
- per month! To top it all, Pamela did not stop at that, she even married
him! He is still alive.

Daughters, Nieces and the likes: Look closely at their hands. You
will find the 'papa' and the 'uncle' closely wrapped around their little
fingers. No matter what he may be, a man has to go by the dictates of his
daughter etc. on what he must wear, eat or even think.

So dear regimental friends, entertain no wrong notions – it is a
female ruled society. Propaganda of the so called 'male domination' is a
deep-rooted conspiracy to keep the gender advantage in women's favour.
So that little girls monopolise on cushy jobs, leaving the tedious and
bloody work for the boys. And so perpetuates the brazen discrimination

for ever. Having *Bhagayeshwari* join the ranks of cannon fodders is therefore a long overdue step towards gender equality – in favour of men.

Even in the matter of warfare, it is *Durga, Kali, Jagdamba*, and later, *Durgawati, Ahilyabai, Lakshmibai*, right down to *Indira Gandhi* and her modestly gifted daughter-in-law, *Sonia ji*, who occupy the place of honour, destroying their opponents, who happen to be men, always and every time.

Here ye all *Hanumans* of FIFTY ONE, tell our soldiers that we now have a resident incarnate of '*shakti*'. She will bring us more victories, again and yet again.

*

17

A 'Prince' in Borewell

The community 'open-well' has ever been a centre of village life in rural India. Even in urban settlements, such wells have invariably been an integral part of a family's residence. Presently, however, with the mounting pressure of high demand for water, the traditional manual well-digging has been replaced with machine-drilling of bore-wells.

In the days of yore, open-wells came in different forms: brick-lined or unlined, with parapet or just level with ground, sign-posted or abrupt. Some were provided with beam-pulley-rope-bucket arrangement to ease the exertion of drawing water, while others were left just with a log thrown across the pit, on which to plant one leg while the other rested on the edge, and so balanced, to pull up the water-filled bucket. A well, in fact, was a sign of the owner's – individual or community – status. It was also a symbol of caste-discrimination, 'lower' castes having been assigned segregated wells to use. That was the scene in most of India, even in the metro cities, till the 1960's or thereabouts. Even today, the scene has not changed much, nearly a billion Indians live on wells, pun intended!

Then there were wells dug by farmers, brick kiln owners and the like – just a big, deep hole in the *terra-firma*, hidden by undulations or undergrowth which abounded across the fields and fallow areas, many of these dry and abandoned. Besides serving their owners, these wells were – and still remain – a major consideration for the planners and participants of military field-training exercises, on occasions to serve parched throats, and to avoid breaking bones of unsuspecting soldiers on others. There also have been instances of wells gobbling up military trucks and even tanks, the victims having to carry the burden of jokes over the rest of their service – and during re-union of veterans thereafter.

Instances of children tumbling into wells has ever been a matter of concern among Indian mothers. With the advent of 'bore-wells', that concern should have been ameliorated, had there been a sense of care to cover the unsuccessful bore's, which outnumber the yielding ones. On the contrary, true to the cliché, "it can happen in India only", children sliding into exposed bore-wells seems to have become an oft repeated feature in rural India. Besides, while pulling out the victim from open-wells was simpler, that is not so with the narrow and deep bore-wells.

It is not known as to when did the first such accident took place, nor is it known as to how many perished, before a daily-wager labourer's son, named 'Prince', fell into one in a non-descript village of Haryana on the afternoon of 21 July 2006.

Four year old Prince of *Haldageri* village near Ambala, while playing at a cross-section of village lanes right in front of the village *Gurudwara*, fell into a 12 inch diameter, 53 feet deep dry and abandoned bore-well – yes, the bore-well was located thus and covered with just a piece of gunny bag! Friends raised alarm and the villagers got activated in deepening an abandoned, dry, 20 feet deep open-well which adjoined the bore-well at just 10 feet away. Of course, even after working overnight, they could make practically no headway. The district police and the collectorate were informed.

In a rare instance of prompt response, the Collector and the Inspector General, accompanied by their subordinate staff had reached the spot within a few hours. Even if the Fire Fighting staff found neither the expertise nor equipment to get into the act, arrangements for pumping oxygen and lowering snacks and juices were rigged up under the supervision of doctors of the civil hospital nearby. Lighting inside the hole – by lowering an electric bulb – and vigil over the boy – by lowering a camera – were soon activated. By late evening, the boy had a lease of life, if only for the time being. The task of extricating him remained daunting and unresolved.

As 'it happens – nay, must happen – in India only', the Army was called out to extricate the victim, the underlying idea being to extricate the civil functionaries from people's ire which in turn could prompt the politicians to indulge in the usual charade of superficial breast-beating. By mid morning, the troops had reached the site while heavy duty cranes, excavators, generators, boring machines and implements etc. fetched up soon enough. Thus while the doctors and fire fighters maintained vigil over the boy, incoherent by this time, the Army Engineers got down to deepening the adjacent open-well. The culture that still survives in villages prompted every one to join up in whatever manner one could, digging, offering drinking water to sweating soldiers and bandaging their injuries, running errands, finding implements – anything that would help. The local Gurudwara became the hub of their efforts.

By now, thanks to an efficient electronic media and its ever-active representatives of various news channels, the BBC and CNN included, who had reached the spot, the news had spread all across India, even abroad. The entire rescue operation was broadcast 'live', as people – the Speaker of Lok Sabha, the Defence Minister, and all hues of politicians, officials, businessmen, professionals and common folk – remained glued to their television sets. Mandirs, masjids, gurudwaras and churches resounded with prayers for the boy while others did that in their homes. It was a situation unseen ever, unprecedented; it brought the nation's diversity to gel into just one cause, so much so that it became mandatory for the people of political eminence, the Chief Minister included, to be seen at the spot, ostensibly sharing the Army's burden. Reporters of channels not represented thus far, were instructed to reach the site *poste-haste*.

As the head of all Army Engineers in the Western Theatre, I decided to stay away and let the team, under an intrepid Captain, do their work unhindered; after all it was a section task, no more could be deployed without spoiling the broth. In any case, the astute Commanding Officer was already at hand to lead and supervise. Army Chief's and Defence minister's call made me realise that more than the operation, it was a matter of managing the sundry's that needed my presence. As I reached the location 100 kilometers away, deepening of the open-well had commenced against the hindrances caused by inquisitive crowds of thousands, politicians and officials dedicated to the camera and many self-certified 'experts' holding forth in front of television cameras to educate the countrymen on various nuances of the episode. It was a charade!

The surging crowd had made the operation dangerous with the possibility of the ground caving in, burying those working underground. Loud proclamations to provide space, made by the Inspector General and the Superintendent of Police, were ignored when they were not being pushed around, and their policemen were struggling to check the push coming from the crowds at the rear. At this instance I requested the Chief Minister to take control and save the situation. *Mr Huda* came to his best: he shouted, caned and rushed at the crowds. The policemen took the lead to join-in and in a matter of minutes, the area was cleared for the Captain to speed up the operation.

As earth was excavated from the open-well, it was lifted out for disposal by improvised buckets held by a crane. Then to prevent cave-in, a tube-like steel-plated caisson, held against inward collapse by spokes of angle iron struts, was inserted into the open-well to hold the earthen wall. As the open-well reached the depth of the bore-well on the morning of 23 July, one part of the operation was over; the next part was even more crucial. A horizontal, three feet diameter tunnel was dug between the two wells along an alignment fixed through laser range-finder. Here was a sandy patch that was liable to collapse, and therefore empty bitumen drums were inserted to line the tunnel. Finally, as darkness fell, the tunnel hit the bore-well. A shout went up; television crews tried to break-in, and finding the policemen in no mood to oblige, started to interview any one who would succumb. Many insinuations were thus broadcast across India, one suggesting that the tunnel had missed the bore-well while the other gave another two hours to get the boy out.

Standing on a earthen mound next to the open-well with the Chief Minister, the local Members of Parliament and state legislature and other actual and pretending VIPs, I had the time to reflect. The entire operation was seen by millions in their televisions, politicians were making statements and hope of rescuing the half-dead boy had soared, much contrary to the situation on ground. The toughest part was yet to come when the boy will have to be pulled out through the narrow tunnel, the fear of its collapse, leading to final burial of both the rescuers and the rescued, looming in my idle mind. Popular expectation having overwhelmed the reality, a failure would hurt the Army's image. More than that, watching my troops engaged regardless, I felt a tinge of sadness. "These fellows deserve success", I thought, "but providence has its own ways!". I prayed that that the boy remains alive – he had been through the trauma for over 50 hours after all.

At long last, after an excruciating crawl through the tunnel, a soldier could catch hold of the boy's arm. But the delirious boy would not move for fear. It was not a place to struggle and therefore the boy's uncle was sent in. The boy, limp and cold, was wrapped in a bed-sheet and brought up by the crane in the arms of the happy Captain. Thousand hands tried to reach out to touch and grab the boy, an aspiring assembly ticket-seeker among them. Fearing that the so far alive fellow would be inadvertently lynched by a doting crowd, I took him and with soldiers clearing the way, marched straight into the Gurudwara to hand over the boy to the Chief Minister.

Then as celebrations, good and boisterous, started, I ordered a return to barracks; the revelry seemed out of sync with the soldiery.

For months on, there was little discussed beyond that rescue operation. Top leaders queued up to congratulate and the press ran after stories, true and speculated. The irksome sequence went on; irksome because there was little done to avoid repetition of that crime – leaving bore-wells open. In later times many children have been lost to that madness.

Irksome also because of the burden of not getting the Commanding Officer his due award rankles me still. It was an event of a decade and besides being a lesson in perseverance and professionalism, brought to the Army such accolades that it had not experienced in recent years. Army brass who remain ensconced in better environs of the South Block, and who liberally bestow awards upon their favourites, however, thought otherwise – or rather did not think of it at all. My entreaties either went unanswered or fruitless in the end.

Evident by being recognised even after many years, the 'Prince' storey rules many hearts even today. That is my homage to those officers and men who worked for it.

*

18

The Final Solution

Shri *Griheraj Katil* rose from his allotted seat among the treasury bench, a sheaf of loose papers in his hand. He adjusted his reading glasses over his sharp nose-ridge, quite unnecessarily, as he dipped his chin and directed his gaze over his glasses to survey the honourable members of the house some of whom were in a state of deep closed-eye contemplation, some transfixed – glazed eyes, open mouth and all as if in a state of post-subsidised lunch stupor – and some whispering among themselves words of extreme national import; some were actually staring back at the honourable minister's lean, tall frame, as if ready to imbibe his statement.

After a seemingly unending pause and just as the suspense was about to cause seizure among the audience – those who were awake – the honourable minister spake. "There is no *Naxal* problem", he stated in his trademark measured tone; 'there are no Naxals", he concluded with a finality that is characteristic of a chief guest of proclaimed 'excellency' announcing closure of an international sports meet.

And how that one-liner – just a statement – changed India !

The Indigenous Followers of Mao (IFM) – since there were no Naxals, that was the only way to describe this lot – were shell shocked.

Their years of effort on perpetrating mayhem and tumult had been reduced to just naught by just one sentence spoken at a far away capital of the 'enemy' class. There was despondency, even dismay, at this pronouncement; some IFM cadres even went to the verge of psychological collapse. "What am I then?, do I exist?, what is to happen to my existence, or was it just an illusion?" ..., each one asked of the other, both gazing vacantly at the infinity, tears rolling down their taut jaws.

A sense of deep confusion and disconcert engulfed the IFM cadres. Some considered calling a 'bundh', others argued rather convincingly that they could not do so, since they just 'did not exist'! A meeting of the politbureau was called but some of the 'non-existent' members asked, "politbureau of what?" There being no answer, the meeting had to be cancelled. A pall of gloom descended upon the forest hide-outs of the IFM hoards. Indeed, the honourable minister had scattered the myth of the Naxals and the existence of the entire lot of the hoards with it. Such strategic *coup de grace* would have made that fellow *Sun Zhu* proud, his singular obsession being in "winning war without having to fight". In the event, however, the honourable minister was sacked while he had retired to change his safari suit for the ninth time on that day.

Worse was yet to come for the IFM. Oppressed by hunger – for a liquid variety of course – some cadres tried to commence their routine 'collection' of 'donations' for the 'cause of the proletariat', a noble deed which the 'class enemies' had mischievously termed as 'nothing but extortion'. But the excursion was of no effect. The truck drivers and petty contractors who were ordained to make the 'voluntary donations' refused point blank. "What are you?", they demanded and remained unmoved to the pathetic entreaties of the Cadres. The Cadres even tried to point guns on these intransigent agents of the bourgeoisie, but these louts laughed it away, "Since you do not exist, you are technically incapable of wielding guns", they argued – very convincingly.

India was transformed overnight. Leaders of the movement – the creed of *Prabir da's* and *Sunil ji's* – returned to the bosom of their city based parents. Presently, many of them were found chatting with their bridal candidates over tea, samosa and gulab jamun, indulgently watched over by the parents on both sides. The Cadres went back to their unemployed days, while some were drafted as coolies by the mineral and forest mafia. Columns of policemen were seen moving about collecting their weapons, which had earlier been looted by the IFM cadres, aided of course by the former's co-operation, and which now lay abandoned in wells and bushes.

At their wit's end, the ideologues – the only variety left in the lurch, they having nowhere to repair to maintain their life style – went to present a memorandum of protest to a more honourable minister of the *mind-pleasing* (man-mohan) variety. They could not. Since they did not exist, no one took them seriously. They were shooed away. Abandoned, unnoticed, unlamented, and thoroughly disgusted with the ways of democracy, these ideologues have taken to singing ballads at market places to earn their bread.

When teased about the regime of extortion, loot and murder having come to an end, and *inter alia*, their days of milk-and-honey being over, the policemen grinned. "Don't be silly. The lot of pseudo-politicians, dubious corporates' and real dacoits have already reinstated themselves. They would do better than the IFM. Our milk-and-honey is guaranteed", they snugly replied.

Eternal India at her supreme best!

*

19

Back to the Bygone

Looking back he found it strange that the most pleasing moments of his life also brought in its wake a whiff of sadness.

Duty had brought him to this outback where he spent his young days – days of silly fears and sillier wants. It was well past noon when the conclave finally ended. By the time he could extricate himself from the numerous courtiers and power-brokers who invariably congregate at such occasions and take leave of the Chief Minister from the luncheon hosted by him, the Sun was turning golden yellow and the usual afternoon calm was getting better of the noise and chaos in the city.

Soon, his cavalcade was streaming over the highway towards his next destination. Golden Sun rays had by now started their eternal frolic with the red earth, its green forests and yellowing patches of paddy fields to transform the country-side with a beauty of indescribable serenity. "I had missed this for so long...!", he mused. He had the air-conditioner turned off and the window glass rolled down. The rush of earth-scented air seemed to blow away his wad of worries and blues. He was back to his school days; he belonged here in those days long past. He recalled those lazy carefree days of innocence. It was so different from what a fifty-plus high official was obliged to live through, bound all the time in procedures, precedence's, programmes and protocols, and perpetually engaged in an unending rat-race with problems found and created in the course of his duties.

He was brought back to reality by the crackle of the radio set. It was announcing that there was a *raasta roko* (block the road) agitation taking place some distance away and that it would take a few hours when the agitating mob, done in by thirst, hunger and hoarse throat, would find some excuse to melt away without, of course, making any difference to the 'cause' of the protest. Pleasantly struck by this unexpected opportunity to look for the once familiar 'Jaina More' – a humble cross roads named after some fellow who no one recalls. His faded memory told him that the *More* would be somewhere around and so he overruled the security officer's suggestion to halt at a nearby dak bunglow.

Even if it was the privileged hub of an unprivileged local life, that spot, Jaina More, was nothing more than a non-descript, inconsequential blot upon the rudimentary landscape. It was a typical cross-road with its regulation cluster of one cycle repair shop, two tea stalls, a *beedi* (a small, locally rolled cigar) seller and one *kirana* (every tit-bit) store, each under make-shift awnings of bamboo and thatch, and crowned with hoardings which displayed rather uncomplimentary imitations of film stars *Dilip Kumar* having his cycles repaired and *Ashok Kumar* puffing on beedi, both grinning ear to ear. From here took off an intimately familiar broken, dusty track that would lead to the village of *Satanpur*, his blissful playground of young days. He decided to look for the landmark.

His watch was soon over. Jaina More had changed but the old, rusty sign boards still hung on, even if consigned in favour of new ones bearing equally uncharitable images of various Bollywood 'Khans' smilingly repeating what the 'Kumars' had been obliged to go through before them. The tea stall had graduated itself to what was ambitiously named as 'Hotel Raj' while it remained little more than a tea-and-samosa corner. The dirt track had been subjected to experimentation with black-topping, obviously at the behest of the local legislator in his attempt to what the politicians nonchalantly describe as "service to the people". Expectedly, the work was executed so tentatively that the top had more potholes and undulations than what could pass as a road surface. "They should have left the old track as it was", he murmured, "official apathy and neglect in the name of development shows more starkly in rural areas". Relief from being tossed about, thankfully, was not much delayed. After disbursement of regulation 'commission' to all and sundry starting from the legislator down to the lowly village headman, little of the fund allocated would have been left, and a kilometre long sample of work having been done, just by the old Siva temple, the black-top disappeared. And so the dirt track reappeared, apparently untouched over many decades past.

Hereafter, the Ambassador car could barely manage to crawl over the narrow strip of track that was unaccustomed in hosting any transport more distinguished than a bullock cart, while elephant grass on either side caressed the car's white body in a gesture of welcome. The caress reminded him of his ever indulgent '*pishi-ma*' (father's sister – English language is so cruel, it fails to annotate the distinct flavours of bondages we Indians have with our streams of uncles, aunts and cousins). Apparently unmindful, pishi-ma would sooth his unruly hair as progressed the after dinner routine of story-telling sessions that featured in the open courtyard under the star studded night sky, a circle of thirty odd children from one to fourteen years of age savouring every word said, every syllable enacted.

A lean, gaunt man in white *kurta-pajama* (indigenous long shirt and loose trousers) hurriedly dismounted from his rickety bicycle to make way for the car. Looking the man over as the car passed by, he instantly realised that he knew the fellow! Thirty five years and many changes in the man's deportment didn't seem to have diminished the latent vibe they had enjoyed once. Yes indeed, this was his 'Gopla'! He had the car stopped and surprised at his own recall, hailed the man as he had done all those years ago; "You goat!", he shouted before alighting and motioning the car to move off to one side. The object of this endearment, Gopla (formally named Gopal, and described by the title 'goat'), glowing in a flicker of recognition, dumped the bike and ran up to hug and lift him off the ground. "You monkey", bellowed the man just as he was wont to in the times gone past.

Pushing the cycle between them, the childhood friends talked and walked over the once familiar surroundings, going past the much venerated football ground of irregular dimensions that left for its players a rather hard, uneven turf and improvised goal-posts – not that any one ever complained. Soon enough, they acquired a following of a score of awe struck bare bodied children in soiled half-pants, some even in simple *chaddhi's* (loin cloth underwear that doubled up as a regular attire), whispering remarks, suggestions and guess work over this contrasting duo. Amused by his own spontaneous behaviour, he found himself a changed man, blabbering, gesticulating, laughing, backslapping, and unmindful of the dots of cow dung strewn about, kicking up dirt with his immaculately polished shoes. He felt at home, and savoured the still familiar smells of the village air, its soil, ponds, bundles of firewood and heaps of cow dung that decorated the open court yards of every mud-and-tile hut. The only object he found unfamiliarity with was the people – he did not know them. He had grown away from those days when as a child, he would accompany his parents to Satanpur during the summer holidays to spend a few unbridled, riotous days with his pishi-ma and her blessed joint family in which flourished thirty odd boys and girls, each unique in demeanour and yet bonded in one tie.

As Gopla went on a non-stop rambling to update him on their friends, accomplishes and acquaintances of younger days, he saw how far his career had moved him away from the simple, earthy surroundings into a surreal world of complexities and compulsions. He could not decide whether it was for the better or worse, yet he felt a tinge of remorse for those days when bliss prevailed uninterrupted and problems were accepted as a bonafide part of life.

"Oh! Kamla di?", Gopla was recounting, "She was married off into the *Ghoshal* family of *Pathuria*. The husband who worked in Calcutta, returned some years later with tuberculosis and died soon after. Presently, her daughter married and settled, Kamla di has returned to tend to her father's farm land. She lives in that same house". As they treaded along the dirt track past the familiar village well, the mango grove and the ageing school building, he learnt that *Debu* was running a grocery shop at a nearby *kasba* (a small town), *Nikhil* had gone on to be a top geologist with the Tata's, *Gandhi* was a machinist in a nearby factory, ... thus continued the stock taking. Sheepishly he found that he could not relate to these buddies anymore. "It somehow isn't the same, I do not know them, we have grown so much apart!", he pondered.

The house had not changed much; Kamla di had. The fair, soft featured and ever indulgent *didi* (elder sister) had turned into a gaunt, heavy and squeamish woman in her struggle to keep up with a life so unforgiving. "Gautam?, who Gautam?", she enquired suspiciously as Gopla presented him to her scrutiny. Realisation soon brought back hints of that serene, welcoming smile – unused as she seemed to be in showing that kind of gesture. As she was wont to with her favourite foster kid-brother, she made unsteady attempts at pampering him with a plate of *moa* (local puffed rice sweet meat) and jaggery, his once favourite munch. But it wasn't the same; it all seemed out of place on this day. The easy bondage had withered away, loved ones had grown out to be strangers, time had taken the sheen out of that pleasant part of life. It was a heartbreak. Yet it did not pinch. There seemed to be an acceptable understanding in him, as in others.

The protocol officer stepped in, "We should be leaving before it is too late to travel in these parts". He looked embarrassed, but yet decided to see, before taking leave, what was once the paradise of his childhood days. They headed towards his long gone pishima's home. The sprawling, brick-and-tile house stood amongst its surrounding grounds just as it was, its symmetry marred somewhat by few newly constructed rooms where a wide veranda – indoor playground for the children – once lay. The decibels of nearly 24x7 shouts, shrieks and the drone of household chores had given way to a quietude that was occasionally interrupted by the rustle of tree leaves. "The property has been divided amongst the family on your pishima's in-law's side", clarified Gopla. "Most have migrated to towns near and afar, only four old couples and a widow live here in their portions of the house. It would be proper for you to meet them", Gopla suggested.

The meeting, with what was then seen as a much envied liberated group of young men for all their smart cloths, wrist watches and college life, was pleasant. Considered as 'distant relatives' in Indian contention, nine faces withered and bodies frail congregated around the seat offered him. Recognition rekindled and gleeful recount of long forgotten tales of his mischief dominated the conversation. With every one warmed up to cross-talk, fact-corrections and loud interruptions over buckets of *jhaal muri* (spiced rice puff) and *moa*, soon the house seemed to have gone back to its riotous days. Laughter had come back, if for a short interlude to lonely lives. That was when the protocol fellow intervened, more firmly this time.

The journey to the 'present' was spent in solicitude. It was filled with kaleidoscopic scenes of past events joyous and heart-rending, and the contrast that the present seemed to show. He was inclined to fall into nostalgia that invariably brings in its wake a sense of loss over the 'change'. Thinking over as to what it would be like if matters remained the same, he couldn't help repudiating that call.

"Things were as these should have been *then*, the present is as it must be", he pondered.

*

20

Understanding Civil-Military Relations

> *"Values necessary to defend the society are often at odds with the values of society itself...Military and Civil can co-exist with different norms of behaviour..."*
>
> —*Gen Walter Kerwin.*

Contortion of a Statutory Relationship

The first decade of the new millennium has seen the management of the Indian military institution through the sanctified process of civilian control marred by serious incongruencies. Thus the hoary relationship between the civil and military institutions of the Indian state apparatus has become contentious to a degree that it can not bode well for the nationhood. The disconnect is exemplified by the armed forces leadership expressing dismay at shortage of battle leadership and deficiencies in war-wherewithal, military personnel vociferously charging the defence bureaucracy of subversion of armed forces' entitlements and protocol, the apex court chastising the government on its maltreatment of the soldiery, veterans returning their medals to the *Rashtrapati* and the Parliament rejecting the government's stance on military pension. Strangely, all this while, the government remains stoically indifferent! The situation is not helped by accusations of conspiratorial subterfuge of the military's interests by a political-bureaucratic nexus. Meanwhile, cases of misconduct amongst the military brass adds to the unholy mess. Notably, each of these misconducts have a civil-military interface, a joint venture of inviting disaster, so to say, in which some military members could not resist the greed of joining their civilian counterparts in perpetuating graft.

Thus goes on a wholly avoidable charade wherein civil institutions, thoroughly discredited already, have nothing to lose, whereas the military institution, seen as the last bastion of honour and professionalism, has much at stake. Most disconcertingly, it is the nation which, in allowing degeneration of one of the few noble institutions of the state, upkeep of which extracts heavy investment of blood, sweat and public money, stands to lose the most: the due *peace-dividend*. No doubt, the situation has caused much dismay among the farsighted and responsible members of our society.

How did the situation turn so suicidal?

The answer lies in lack of understanding – by innocence or design, or both – of the sanctified nuances of *'Civil-Military Relationship'* in a democracy. No doubt, there is inadequate appreciation of this subject even among the military fraternity that causes them to treat war-fighting as a burden of the military alone and so accept below-par response to defence requirements from civil institutions. But since the reins of this crucial facet of state-craft is held by nation's civilian leadership, its vitiation must be seen as a failing of the Indian system of military management. That the nation will have to pay dearly for this self-infliction, is a disturbing thought indeed.

But to appreciate the imperative of true understanding, it is necessary to delve into defining as to what really is implied by 'Civil-Military Relationship' in the construct of a sovereign state.

The Statute of 'Civil-Military Relations'

Factually considered, 'Civil-Military Relationship' is about committing national resources in winning wars. It is a sublime aspect of state-craft that nurtures its soldiery and ordains them to undertake extra-ordinary sacrifices for the greater good of the society, while subordinating all civilian resources to the war-effort. This pristine relationship, therefore, is not about the machinations that go on in South Block to keep the military hierarchy at the mercy of civil servants in the pretext of maintaining civil supremacy.

Political philosophers point to two distinct constituents of the relationships between civil and military institutions of a nation-state. These are:

- The State-Military Contract, and
- The Society-Soldier Covenant.

These aspects call for some discussion.

The State-Military Contract

War is the ultimate recourse of a state to protect its interests when all other less extreme methods fail. Its centrality in state-craft falls out of the fact that in the international arena, there being no statutory laws nor any law enforcement mechanism, articulation of military force remains the sole arbitrator in prevailing upon belligerent states or groups. Indeed, there are certain consensual 'laws' and 'conventions' – laws of seas, Geneva Convention, Mine Protocol etc. – but these are not binding, are seldom enforceable and routinely flouted. The international anarchy is further exacerbated by the fact that even if it takes two to fight, one is enough to start it arbitrarily. Political pundits, from *Plato* to *Morgenthau*, have therefore spelt out the basic ingredients of a sovereign nation-state as, a defined territory to sustain a population, a system of governance and the power to protect its concerns. The interdependency of the state and its military institution therefore needs to be clearly understood and preserved, for it will be fiddled with at the nation's peril.

Political philosophy dictates that it is the for the civilian leadership to decide as to the structure of armed forces it should have, what its mandate should be, and accordingly, what kind of best organisation, weapons and equipment need to be placed at its disposal. To elaborate the last aspect, the 'state-military contract' signifies a sacred commitment from the state to ensure that the soldiery is best geared up in terms of weapons, equipment, training, state-support and above all, motivation and morale, to be able to plunge into the dangerous mandate with good chances of success and survival. This is a pledge eternally sanctified by a responsible state.

As a corollary, it is for the military institution to ensure, regardless, that the political mandate is fulfilled in the most effective manner and with least of societal devastation. Accordingly, soldier's commitment to the state entails highest degree of professionalism, ingenuous orchestration of war-wherewithal, perfection in training, and above all, a sacrament of 'duty over death'. Indeed, this is an extra-ordinary mutuality of implicit trust, a sort of pious vow of temporal solidarity. That is why nations go to the extent of cutting their basic needs to equip their soldiery, and that is why soldiers plunge into deprivation and death while other citizens may take to flight. The spirit behind this 'contract' is best summarised when President Eisenhower reiterated what Kautilya had stated two thousand years ago, "*When diplomats fail to maintain peace, the soldier is called upon to restore peace. When civil administration fails to maintain order, the soldier is called to restore order. As the nation's final safeguard, the army cannot afford a failure in either circumstances. Failure of army can lead to national catastrophe, endangering the survival of the nation*". It is on this account that up from the smallest detachment to the highest seat, armed forces have to be manned with highly professional and motivated soldiers, for mistakes military have severe and perpetual ramifications. Further, while it takes decades to build up a military institution, it takes generations to foster soldierly culture. It is on this accord that nations that are gifted with wisdom and foresight take their military institution very, very seriously.

One is not sure if civilians, or even the soldiers, recognise this over-arch of the 'state-military contract' in its sublime perspective and understand as to why the services are accorded special status in informed societies, as to why military leaders are '*commissioned*' by the state, not merely 'inducted' or 'appointed', and unique recourses – some privileged, some harsh – are applied to administer the military institution.

In tangible terms of the 'state-military contract', special provisions are instituted for the soldiers to be drafted young, kept young, subjected to strict rules, expected to set higher standards of professionalism and probity, and tested at every stage before being selectively promoted. Provisions are also made for the nation's civilian sector to accord priority response to the requirements of the armed forces through stipulations of the 'Union War Book', 'emergency schemes' at state and district levels, enforcement of 'defence restrictions' over sensitive matters and 'guaranteed reserves' of support resources – food, fuel, manpower, transport, equipment, technicians etc. Administrative priority is also provisioned through the 'Civil-Military Liaison Meetings', the 'Cantonment Act', land notifications and protection of military requirements – like weapons, ammunition, rations, emoluments etc. – under the budgetary practice of 'first charge'.

As it will be seen later, the Indian state has, in some ways, been unable to uphold the sanctity of 'state-military equation'; that failure has exposed chinks in its wisdom.

The discussion may now turn to the second constituent of the 'Civil-Military Relations', that is, the ever-sacrosanct 'society-soldier covenant'.

The Society-Soldier Covenant

Warfare is characterised by ultimate use of constitutionally sanctified violence, wherein soldiers are called upon to overcome the core human instincts of self-preservation, comfort and profit, and so to stand up to extreme hazards of death, deprivations and destruction on their line of duty. Another notable soldierly attribute is that while the common man observes societal rules to be safe, the soldier commits to an altruistic mandate that requires him to engage in extreme exactions. This he does for *honour* – the Army Act or remuneration cannot motivate a soldier to stake his life. 'Civil-Military Relationship' is thus anointed by a sublime form of 'society-soldier covenant'. Obviously, the 'covenant' is bound by moral considerations; its plank is spiritual, not merely material or legal.

The 'society-soldier covenant' rests on recognition that the profession of arms differs from all others in every aspect, as manifested in unique nuances of recruitment, psychological conditioning, service conditions, training, discipline, distinct culture and ethos, and suspension of fundamental citizenry rights. This 'covenant' enjoins the soldier to give up many of his intrinsic human concerns in favour of protecting the security and honour of the society. In reciprocal vein, the 'covenant' also stipulates, firstly, that the society is morally bound to accord unstinted support to the soldier for him to undertake his mission free from non-military concerns, and secondly, that rewards of the soldiers' 'calling' are to be measured against compensation for hardships, abrogation of freedom and commitment to stand fast, die for that matter, when it is permissible for every citizen to scoot, hide or submit. The 'covenant' also extends exclusive constitutional enactments to the benefits of the soldiery in terms of litigious and penal code dispensations, land allotment, various grants, welfare schemes, and so on. By far the most remarkable constitutional provision made for the soldiery are, firstly, the right to be 'judged' by their own fraternity, and secondly, convergence of legislative, executive and judicial powers at the hands of the sole commander – in rest of the state apparatus these are purposefully segregated. These are landmark provisions which distinguish the soldiers' 'calling' above the rest.

Manifestation of the 'society-soldier covenant' thus boils down to the soldier's unbound commitment, and its grateful recognition in the society by way of bestowal of singular honour upon him. It is a matter of satisfaction that this 'covenant' is honoured by every citizen of India when he routinely extends out-of-turn considerations to his soldiery. In 1962, troop's acceptance of the political imposition in engaging in hopeless fight at the *Namka Chu*, and the entire nation's deeply aggrieved eulogium in repenting the neglect of its soldiery, are examples of the spirit that guides this 'covenant'. No doubt, with the rise of unbound materialism of the modern times, the 'covenant' has seen dilutions at the hands of power-brokers and moolah-worshipers; yet the *aam Bharatiya* and his society remains steadfast in his respect for his *fauzi jawan*.

Reality Check

To summarise, 'Civil-Military Relations' is at the root of the age-old dictum of state-craft that recognises the military as an unique institution, fundamentally different from civil way of life, which it is mandated to protect by recourse to articulation of force. As a corollary, the state is bound to administer its armed forces according to norms and practices that are profoundly distinct from civil-specific measures. No doubt, breach of this hallowed principle of governance must invite disaster.

It will be interesting see as to how well this principle is in force in India.

As one party to the 'Civil-Military Relations', it is apparent that baring freak exceptions, the military institution in India has scrupulously adhered to its role in the 'state-military contract' as well as the 'society-soldier covenant'. Marginalised in the newly independent India, it nevertheless held the country together in 1947-48 against tribal invasion of J&K and the horrific partition riots, and put up fierce resistance to the Chinese juggernaut in 1962 even when bereft of bare essentials of war-wherewithal. When adequately provided for between 1965 and 1990, it was eminently successful in backing up the nation's political goals, internal and external. Subjected to stagnation once again during the years following, it fought back to reclaim its honour in Kargil and reinforced Indian diplomacy through 'Operation Parakram'. Alongside these events, the military institution has preserved India's integrity against a succession of vicious insurgencies, earned international recognition in UN Missions and devoted itself in rescue and relief during national calamities – all more or less without a break during the six decades of independent India. Above all, it has conducted itself honourably within the democratic, societal and humane norms, never failing to correct stray cases of misdemeanour. No wonder then that the nation sees its military institution as one of the few that continues to stand tall.

As the prime-mover of Civil-Military Relationship, the Indian state has attended well to its soldiery's professional, social and domestic needs to the extent practicable within the systemic dispensation. The Indian soldier eats, dresses and lives well, has the best of medical attention and is able to nurture his family. The military service remains attractive and the soldiers are a well respected and satisfied lot at the end of their service. Truly, the nation pulled out all stops in supporting the armed forces during the mobilisations in 1965, 1971, Sri Lanka, Kargil and Operation Parakram, as it does during the major manoeuvres. Similarly, state governments too take much pride in finding ways to meet the requirements of the armed forces. Besides, in such rare instances when the military institution has slipped up in its duty – the intrusion in Kargil, for example – the state has stood up to protected its image. However, in many other aspects, the state has deviated from the sanctified part of its 'relationship' and, in some ways, failed its military institution. Manifestation of this failure is seen in the Defence Ministry's nonchalant approach to comprehensive modernisation of the military establishment, delays in procurements and execution of strategic projects and failure to attract competent volunteers into junior leadership.

Some of the debilitating failings of the state, in contravention of its sanctified role in 'state-military contract' raise serious concerns. The crucial ones among these may be recounted here.

One, while the entire government machinery has opened up to promote initiative, expertise, delegation, modernisation, re-structuring and modern management practices, the Ministry of Defence remains frozen in its post-independent fixations. Here, bureaucrats, scientists and auditors – all innocent of military matters – have to decide as to what is needed to keep the military institution in fighting fettle while the military hierarchy is kept at an arm's length. Thus while most routine and mundane proposals require their penny-counting 'scrutiny' and 'approval', unfamiliarity with the larger issues – like nuances of warfare, restructuring, equipment profiling, strategic infrastructure etc.- causes these hapless power centres to dither endlessly. The result is a stagnant military organisation that belies the concept of cost-effective 'military-dividend' to the nation.

Two, the damage done to the military interface in defence-dedicated civilian establishments like the Department of Defence Estates, Military Engineering Service and the Defence Research & Development Organisation (DRDO) is another example of the state's failure to preserve the interests of the military institution. The first two are civilian departments mandated to protect the interests of the armed forces, and accordingly, are subordinated to policies of the designated military authority; President of a Cantonment Board has to be a military officer for example. However, over the years, following repeated upgrades of civilian posts, misleading claims of 'equivalency' of protocol are cited to bypass the sole stake holder, while channels of reporting have been contorted to release these departments from accountability to the military officer. In the case of the DRDO, it is probably the only defence research organisation in the world which is marked by absence of military officers at the decision making level; no wonder that all their projects remain at half-way stage for decades. No doubt, the constituency of civil servants in the Ministry are complicit in this affair. It is also noteworthy that all instances of malpractices that came to the fore recently, are rooted in such departments, even if the military is the first to be targeted.

Three, strategic projects – road construction, land notification, procurements, contracts etc. – have to adhere to civil-specific stipulations; there is no dispensation, no priority for strategic sensitivity. Thus projects languish, costs go up, soldier's hardships rise and strategy stagnates. For example, in strategic road building, it is the military's burden obtain a plethora of 'clearances' from all and sundry agencies, each of these resisting tooth and nail, as if it was only the military's burden to promote national strategy. Absurdity also reigns when procurement of much needed weapon and equipment is held up to avoid allegations of money making by political parties and shady 'syndicates'. Here again, the soldier must bear the burden of systemic probity.

No doubt, on many substantial issues of 'Civil-Military Relations', the state has not been unable to maintain the sanctity of its commitments.

As for the 'societal-soldiery covenant', the situation brings much satisfaction. The common citizen holds his soldiery in very high esteem, so much so that demonstratively paying homage local soldier's sacrifices has become an obligatory performance for the politicians and officials – not in pious solidarity, but in fear of the people's ire. Even in the self-serving officialdom, as also amongst the various wheeler-dealers, soldiers are accorded out of turn considerations. If such special assistances may not be of the extent given earlier, that should be understandable in view of the attributes of the present society. Indeed, there have been slippages in responding to soldiers problems by the civil administration, but such situations have not gone beyond amelioration. Generally, therefore, this aspect of 'Civil-Military Relations' has held its part of the bargain.

At this stage, the focus may be shifted to touch upon the recent trend of growing acrimony between the defence bureaucracy and the armed forces hierarchy, which casts a shadow upon the 'Civil-Military Relationship'.

Defence Bureaucracy and the Military Hierarchy

Recently, vociferous allegations of partisan conduct of the successive 'Pay Commissions' and the unilateral endorsement of discriminatory provisions by the Government has cast a shadow over the 'Civil-Military Relations'. Though actually a matter of base attributes of arrogance, jealousy, fear and malafide grip over power-brokerage at the South Block, it may yet be appropriate to discuss this aspect of the subject under discussion.

No other issue but the systemic undermining of the status and emoluments of the soldiery has, since independence, more besmirched the relationship between the bureaucrats and armed forces officers. Indeed, the former are seen as the villain of this unfortunate episode, somewhat unfairly because while they did process the deliberations, decisions were that of the politicians; the excuse that politicians might have been gullible does not really hold when seen in light of their single-minded articulation of self-agenda. Simply put, in what is somewhat justifiably charged as 'cheating' soldiers of their due, the Pay Commissions have excluded any member from the armed forces – the largest body of affected state officials – and in callous acts of insensitivity, ended up every time downgrading the soldier's emoluments, and by default, his protocol. In previous occasions, soldiers, guided by their pristine ethos, had not looked for any 'tricks' played upon them; when they did this time, it was found that the process of undermining had started decades earlier! The Government was aplomb in dismissing the protests, as it was in avoidance of the judicial reliefs granted in favour of servicemen. Indeed, the perception – and perception matters, right or not – of the Government's nonchalance, and the bitterness it has generated among the soldiery, will take a long time to repair. Adverse fallout on motivation of the soldiery, as manifested by the unfortunate spectacle of veterans returning their war medals to the *Rashtrapati*, must remain as an unprecedented slur on any democratic regime. This situation therefore is a matter of deep concern to all right thinking citizens.

Truly, it is disconcerting to watch our highly competent civil servants and their equally wise political leaders getting into the business of creating demons of themselves in the eyes of the soldiery as much as in the eyes of common citizens. It would therefore be in order to conclude this discussion with the causes of unsavoury disconnect between the defence bureaucracy and the military hierarchy.

Genesis of '*Kalidasa*' Syndrome

At the dawn of independence, India found a group of eminent personalities at the helm of affairs who, notwithstanding their intellect, were novices in management of the military institution. Thus having inherited a highly professional military institution, the politicians had to fall back upon a set of empirical advice rendered by the departing imperialists to administer it. Similarly, the already entrenched civil servants came to be depended upon for defence policy formulation and its implementation. Indeed, the imperialist's advice was burdened with the latent reason for the British to leave: the question of loyalty of the Indian armed forces and a fear of repeat of 1857. In similar vein, civil servants, obliged to remain beholden to the military hierarchy between the two World Wars, resolved to never let their prominence in power-brokerage be challenged ever again. Government of India thus started its independent military management under an influence of suspicion and fear of the military hierarchy. It did make a show of nurturing the defence sector, but down the succeeding years, and particularly following the debacle of 1962, it became apparent that the Indian state had failed this extraordinary institution of its nationhood.

Having learnt the lesson in 1962, the state spared no recourse in strengthening its military institution. Soon, the Defence Ministry, under the leadership of Y B Chavan and Jagjivan Ram, had resuscitated the ill-equipped, ill trained and ill-treated armed forces into a war-winning machine. That effort continued to bear good politico-diplomatic dividends till the late 1980's. During these years, civil servants of the Defence Ministry were revisited on two occasions by the World War-like situation when they were put to the sidelines by *Sam Maneckshaw* and *Sunderji*. The old resolve to undermine the military hierarchy was resuscitated thus. Few civil servants did rise above the petty machinations, *K Subrahmanyam* for example; but they were out of the bureaucratic power-loop.

By 1990, the political complexion had reversed. Within the next five years or so, the military institution was put to such dire straits that the then Army Chief, while making a customary presentation to the Prime Minister, had to rue that the force's "spirit is intact but the body is weak"! Kargil War and 'Operation Parakram' followed that squeezed out what limited weapons, equipment and budgetary options the armed forces still had. All this while the Army was more or less continuously – and successfully – engaged in counter-insurgency operations to preserve the integrity of the nation; that success might have fed the political leadership with a notion that 'all is well' with the military structure.

Today, the armed forces in general and the army in particular is but a listless organisation that, in its traditional die-hard wont, valiantly continues sustains itself with obsolete structure, debilitating deficiencies in battle leadership as well as competent soldiery – both in qualitative and quantitative terms – and of course, mounting shortages in weapons, ammunition and war-like equipment. This, in spite of the nation spending in the upward of rupees two lakh crore annually on her armed forces. How did the state apparatus, a repository of wisdom, land up emulating *Kalidasa*, the original fool who was found sawing the branch he sat upon? Will the state emulate his second coming when he laboured to elevate to such literary excellence as to be the greatest poet of medieval India? Of course, the state can, if it seeks the wisdom of understanding the military institution. For that, the policy-makers have to appreciate the subtle nuances of military management that they read of *Rudolph Holsti, Winston Churchill* and *Samuel Huntington*; these treatise are comprehensible only if tempered with the benefit of understanding the military way of life.

Professional jealousy of the armed forces' top brass – not the soldiery *per se* – among civil servants is an eternal fact since the times of *Talleyrand*. Excellent professionals themselves, nothing rattles them more than the awe-inspiring presence of be-decorated military officers; nothing pleases them more than having such smart and confident officers seek their favour, of which there are always good numbers. It taxes their intellect to administer a highly complex – and unfamiliar – military institution, which they generally manage to do well after much exactions. Professional rivalry, however, may not come in way of deeper understanding of the military institution among those ensconced within the hallowed precincts of the South Block. Policy-makers should be wise to the fact that deficiencies in wherewithal of war is a serious concern while damage to the fabric of military culture is a disease of catastrophic dimensions – not for the soldiery but for the nation.

Adverse effects of superficial understanding of the military institution and mind-sets of cadre-rivalry may not therefore be allowed to impinge upon 'Civil-Military Relations'.

Last Words

It may be appreciated that culturally, strategic articulation of armed might does not figure in India's political agenda. A prerogative of nation's civilian leadership, this policy is to be respected. What however needs to be appreciated by the polity is that the fundamentals of 'Civil-Military

Relationship' must be upheld at all times, else the damage to the military institution will live for generations. That would bring detriment to the society.

It is time for the national leadership to educate themselves.

"*...a permanent piece of education...*", Pandit Nehru, referring to the defeat in 1962.

*

21

Marhaura

Set in the midst of typical rural India, *Marhaura* was like a reflection of an English county even in the post-independence days. It was a happy destination of my school holidays, to be with my family. Father was the head policeman in that part of Bihar's *Chhapra* district. In 1962, the state still retained the grand vestiges of British administration and the concept of law, order and accountability had not yet been consigned to 'democratisation', if the free-for-all that goes on today may be so described.

In the early part of the Twentieth Century, Marhaura, located at the heart of a rich sugar-cane belt of North Bihar, had attracted the attention of Calcutta based *Marwari* industrialists who put up a large sugar factory here. A narrow gauge railway was laid across the endless expanse of sugar cultivations for the 'toy' train to chug over, pulling match-box like open wagons brimming with bundles of sugar-cane that had been collected straight from the fields to be delivered for the factory to take over the processing. Soon, a *pucca* road and metre gauge rail line connected this outback to Chhapra and thence by 'steamer service' to Patna across the serene course of the *Ganges* – imperatives of marketing took care of that. But then there were many like Marhaura in the Gangetic Plains, what was then so special about it?

The answer comes from one Mr *Morton*, bearing whose name came up another sprawling factory to produce the delectable 'Morton Toffee' and its worthy co-product, the 'Milkmaid' brand of condensed milk – globalisation has been a time-immemorial urge, today's whiz-kids might note. Soon, Morton chocolates, in its range of shapes, sizes and formulations, and the sensationally sweet Milkmaid condensed milk in its brand manifestation of an image of an apron-clad woman beaconing the patrons from the tin-wrapping, occupied the dreams of all young Indians – even many not-so-young ones. Indeed, owning a tin-box of Morton toffees, printed with pleasing images of European landscapes, became a treasure among the children, to be possessed and used to keep pencils, marbles and such ingredients of growing up. Even grown ups found use for it. It appeared, wrongly of course, that the products found demand as much for the contents as for usefulness as a container of nick-knacks. Marhaura thus became a centre for sugar and sweet-meat.

As facilities and attractions developed, an 'Iron & Steel Works' came up too. Then came up ancillary workshops, long rows of worker's colonies, thriving markets, schools, clinics and a cinema hall, while the bus stop became a 'bus stand' and the railway siding morphed into a 'station' with all its usual trappings including a *tonga* stand. What distinguished Marhaura, however, was its sprawling bunglows which housed the very British managers and the lot of 'brown sahib' managers-in-the-making. There were also the nice county houses of the Anglo-Indian and purely native supervisors and foremen, each with its flower-filled gardens and lawns. Wide tree lined roads and parks added to raise the status of this once sleepy village as did a football field, few tennis and badminton courts and most importantly, a cricket field – 'The Oval', if you will.

There was a Gymkhana Club open to the *sahibs* and government officials, where liveried staff waited upon the members, who as a matter of faith nurtured few pegs of hard drinks and shuffled with a game or two of cards before proceeding to dine over the 'continental menu'. Ladies chattered in their own circle, joining their men at dinner before vanishing dutifully for the men-folk to lounge into the 'smoke room' – to gossip, and obviously, to smoke cheroot. And of course, needless to mention, there had to be a 'Bengali Club' to give expression to the quintessential Bengali Babu's, their 'misses' and progenies' irrepressible urge to sing, dance, recite and paint at the slightest provocation. The Indian New Year, the first day of *Baishakh* month, was the main occasion for these amateur *shilpis* (artistes), genuine or self-proclaimed, to display such talents that they had to nurture as an act of faith. Then there were the festivities of the *Burra Din* (Christmas), *Durga Puja* and *Diwali*, each celebrated in sublime fervour. Cricket matches in the winters with teams coming from Patna, Chhapra, Darbhanga and Muzaffarpur, football tournaments during the rains, and tennis and billiard 'challenge cups' in between, completed the picture of an oasis of style and affluence that Marhaura was.

The sense of well being had spilled into the local life too. This was reflected in display of bi-cycles, radio sets and modern attire. Prosperity had also found wider following for the local deity, *Garhwa Devi* (deity of the fort). With increasing roll of worshippers, a *pujari ji* (priest) had appeared while the fame of Garhwa Devi's benevolence had spread far and wide. An annual *mela* (religious fair) on the occasion of the *Chhath* festival was a big event at the deity's abode, in which people of all villages around participated. The *Devi's* residence, situated over a mound – probably the site of an ancient *Garh* (fort) – and sheltered by a set of twin trees had been built up to a small enclosure, walled all around and a thatch roof erected to relieve *Her* from the elements. As a nine year old, I had once called on the *Devi* and assigned to her the duty of protecting my father from all those dacoits who seem to bump into him with worrying frequency.

Then, it seems, 'time' took over.

Fifty years after I had said good bye to Marhaura, and having hung my uniform after forty years in the Army, I found the opportunity I had longed for – see and savour the pristine ambience of Marhaura. I knew, of course, that Morton chocolates and the Milkmaid condensed milk had been pushed out of market and that had caused the most colourful gentry of Marhaura to pack bags. Still, I looked for sign of the town's past glory while taking measure of the changes brought about by modernity and development in rural India. More importantly, I had to thank Garhwa Devi. For many times in my younger days, when I found myself boxed-in by debilitating circumstances, I had invoked her blessings, promising to visit her some day to thank her if she complied. My dear class fellow, Jai Prakash Narain Singh, who had recently retired from the Indian Police Service, offered to join me.

The road from Chhapra was wide and smooth; the drive was less so, what with bullock carts ambling over in perfect nonchalance, self-driven by well groomed beasts while the *garhwan* (driver) dozed unconcerned. Erstwhile footpaths to the villages on either side having graduated to dirt tracks, in many cases even to paved village roads, road intersections – *churaha* or *more* in local parlance – appeared every few kilometres. Given over to over-crowding of shops and people, such *churahas* presented chaotic scenes of commuters, vendors, mongrels and various modes of transport jostling about in accompaniment of a persistent drone of cacophony. Of course, that was not an issue if one could ignore the ground rules which gave the right of way, or the 'right' of just standing and observing the life pass by, to curious customers, gossiping clusters, cyclists, proud commuters of 'Vickram' auto-rickshaws and the less numerous but more boisterous owners of motor cycles.

The green country side was as sublime as miles of healthy, wavering rice fields could ever be. There was a massive railway factory coming up, thanks to *Laloo Yadav*, the maverick Bihar politician, I was informed. The once open and inviting entrance to the town, however, had become much constricted by the mingling of scores of push cart-vendors who had taken post over what little was left of the road berms after the permanent shops had claimed their share of encroachments. Then came the *bazaar*, a street overflowing with shops and more vendors, many of them opting to display their wares on mats spread over what little space that their push-cart peers had left for them. The once tree lined avenue had turned into a business street of least order and lesser elegance.

There were many other signs of development. 'International Public

Schools' functioning from 'premises' made up of two room and a veranda, graffiti extolling the virtues of *nari shiksha* (female literacy), 'Aanganvadi' (mother and child care) clinics and sign boards announcing farmers' co-operatives pointed to the fact that rural India was well informed of the societal nuances of the modern era. The *Panchayat* (village Council) had found a roof, rather than the traditional banyan tree, to congregate under, while a row of fruit-sellers did brisk business; obviously, the rural folk could afford fruits, something that was unthinkable in the past. Notably, there were practically no mud huts, all dwellings were of cement-and-brick construction howsoever rudimentary or make-shift these might be. Rural India seemed to be shining. That, however, was not so for the industry in Marhaura.

Our first stop was the deputy police superintendent's office. Marhaura, it transpired, had graduated from being just a *Thana* (police station), to a 'Circle' and thence to a 'Sub-division', though the powers-that-be did not consider it necessary to raise the corresponding facilities like offices, staff, accommodation, transport or communication. Indeed, a sensitive matter like this had to be tackled by the police boss himself; he did so by commandeering the irrigation department guest house. Later, it turned out to be a very fine arrangement and much to every one's benefit. The irrigation department, having given up on reclaiming their possession, demanded rental claims, not too emphatically though, it transpires. The police department ignored the demand. Meanwhile, the policemen found agreeable accommodation and the caretaker found 'understanding' patrons who looked the other way while he leased the land to vegetable growers, looking the 'right' way, of course, when time came to share the 'profit'. The smart and young police boss, barely able to clock his arrogance with hospitality, gave us lunch, cooked at great peril, as he explained, the day being a holiday. He then proceeded to rue his poor luck in having twice qualified for the all-India Indian Police Service and yet not finding place in the merit list, and thus having to settle for the state cadre service, which, he made no bones about, he considered below his station. Then, in his obvious urge to be rid of us, he deputed a guide to take us around.

As the days of new economic regime dawned, the industry, working on dated technology and old business practices, gradually found it tough to remain viable. Worse, it found no one willing, or able, to invest in upgrading the manufacturing units; profits having already been raked in, who after all would open purse to spend on ventures of uncertain future just to keep an English county in India alive. Gradually, all the three manufacturing giants ceased operation. Clubs closed down, toy train was junked and celebrations, 'variety programmes' (singing-dancing-reciting-eating festivals) and sports tournaments ceased. Workers, left in the lurch, encroached upon what premises they could find and stole what could be lifted and sold for profit.

There wasn't much to be taken around. We could barely locate the once majestic factory gates, now fallen and vandalised. The bunglows lay abandoned and crumbling, the rows of cottage type quarters were either dilapidated or taken over by squatters, or both, and cattle rather than players patronised the sports fields. The fate of the club houses, once alive with chatter and activity, was worse; with the gardens gone and bricks, roof tiles and steel members stolen, these looked forlorn and devastated.

It was with some difficulty that I could identify the quarters we had lived in. Its portico had fallen off, the sheet iron roof had been blown away, a portion of wall had collapsed and the ruin, covered with a thick coat of dust, was engulfed with weeds. Even then it was not difficult to recall a picture of our bed room with its high and tall bedstead that was my elder sister's domain, and the open court-yard, centred around which revolved the domestic routine, mother presiding. I could see the spot where, under a hay stack, I had found accommodation for my lovable 'Kutia' (a bitch, literally, who was very fond of me and actually conversed with me, in her own lingo, of course) and her pups till they grew up and went about claiming their over-lordship across the area. New quarters had come up at the spot that had served as our private cricket, football or *gilli-danda* (simple rural sport of despatching a bail-like piece with the strike of a wicket-like baton) pitch. A three storey 'pigeon hole' type staff quarters, with all its seepage, vegetation growth and broken window panes, occupied that spot; it was unlikely to have improved the inmate's living.

Father's old office did little better. Even if in no better condition, it was still in use simply because there was no alternative; it was difficult though to visualise my father working there. The chain-link fencing all around, backed up with neat row of hedges, had vanished, bequeathing its memory to a few iron pickets that had once supported it. The once blooming flower beds were occupied by fifty odd 'case-related' motor bikes, rusting and rotting away in the face of our slow judicial process. The constables' barracks were little better than ruins, dark, dirty, peeling and musty, but yet lived in. The narrow gauge rail line at the rear of the compound had been ripped out, faint signs of its raised embankment still discernible, and the sugarcane fields stood empty and forlorn baring few patches where other type of cultivations went on. The contrast with beaming political, trade and private premises was so prominent – maintaining the police stations in proper trim was obviously not a priority in this state.

It was now the time to bid a final good bye to Marhaura – a repeat visit in my life-time was unlikely. We drove to Garhwa Devi's abode. A majestic gate of polished marble had been erected at the entrance and a row of *pucca* shops had been built on one side – thanks to a devoted Sub Divisional Officer, as the *purohit ji* (the head priest) explained. The *Devi* and her twin trees had a sanctum sanctorum built around them which in turn was situated within a large temple complex with its well maintained rest areas, *havan* (ritualistic invocation) areas and so on. It was a serene and happy place. I thanked *Garhwa Devi* for having kept my father safe from dacoits, besides keeping me from being overwhelmed by troubles all these years. And then we took *Her* leave.

The return journey was covered in reminiscence. Having learned over my life time that whatever exists is what ought to be for the best, I felt joy at the societal developments, just as I happily reconciled with the 'good old days' gone into oblivion. Thus I responded when Jai Prakash enquired as to how the experience was.

*

INDEX